Conversations With My Heart

Conversations With My Heart

Contemplations on God and the World

By Metropolitan Anastasy (Gribanovsky)
Biography by Archbishop Averky (Taushev)

Translated from the Russian by Nicholas Kotar
Edited by Holy Trinity Monastery

HOLY TRINITY PUBLICATIONS
The Print Shop of St Job of Pochaev
Holy Trinity Monastery,
Jordanville, New York
2019

Printed with the blessing of His Eminence,
Metropolitan Hilarion First Hierarch
of the Russian Orthodox Church Outside of Russia

PRINTSHOP OF
SAINT JOB OF POCHAEV

An imprint of

HOLY TRINITY PUBLICATIONS
Holy Trinity Monastery
Jordanville, New York 13361-0036
www.holytrinitypublications.com

ISBN: 978-0-88465-472-8 (paperback)
ISBN: 978-0-88465-425-4 (ePub)
ISBN: 978-0-88465-426-1 (Mobipocket)

Library of Congress Control Number: 2018912202

Cover Design: James Bozeman.
Cover Art: Portrait in oil and watercolor by Archimandrite Cyprian (Pyzhov)

Originally published in Russian in Belgrade in 1935. The second Russian edition,
Беседы с собственным сердцем, was printed from the linotype
in 1948 by Holy Trinity Monastery, Jordanville, NY. 978–0-88465–225-0.
The third edition in Russian was published in 1998.

CONTENTS

INTRODUCTION

In 1998, we celebrated the 125th anniversary of the birth of His Beatitude Metropolitan Anastasy, the second First Hierarch of the Russian Church Abroad. To commemorate this anniversary, we prepared for publication [in the Russian language] his most well-known book—*Conversations With My Heart*. Vladyka Anastasy himself wrote that this book is, as it were, a part of his soul. This edition also includes a short biography of Metropolitan Anastasy, written by another well-respected hierarch of our Church—Archbishop Averky.

We have added a third flower to this holy bouquet of Russian hierarchs. Here we append the words of the recently canonized St John of Shanghai and San Francisco, spoken in 1963 on the occasion of the ninetieth birthday of Metropolitan Anastasy:

> You are the last living member of the Most Holy Synod, presided by the Patriarch, that was chosen by the Moscow All-Russian Council in 1917. You are the only representative of the last legitimate ecclesiastical structure that had undisputed authority over the entire Russian Church. Truly you have the right to speak on behalf of the entire Russian Orthodox Church, not only the Church Abroad … All of us, your nearest colleagues and helpers, feel our insufficiency next to you, and we consider ourselves mere children before you, for you were already a bishop when we were still in school. We assure you of our faithfulness and readiness to help you bear the omophorion of the First Hierarch of the Russian Church Abroad. May the Lord God find you worthy to ascend the heavenly Mount Tabor, where you will eternally witness the uncreated, eternal light of the Life-creating Trinity." (*Pravoslavnaia Rus'*, N° 16, 1963)

We, the children of the Russian Church, believe that the words of St John (Maximovich) of Shanghai and San Francisco came true. And today, the soul of Vladyka Anastasy has passed into the holy mansions of the Most-Holy Trinity, while his body rests (in Holy Trinity Monastery in Jordanville, NY) in anticipation of the coming of the Lord.

Archbishop Laurus
with the brethren of Holy Trinity Monastery
1998

Editor's Note: The translator and editors did not always have access to the same editions of the Russian-language books used by the author. Furthermore, not all of these works exist in English translation, and where they do it is not always possible to cite a corresponding reference. In addition, the author followed a Russian cultural and intellectual practice in which it is not considered essential to give all details of the source material but simply an indication of its origins. Therefore, the notes at the end of this English edition are listed to facilitate the reader's understanding or indicate as closely as possible a source for further reading and study.

PREFACE

> I considered the days of old, and remembered the years of ages
> past, and I pondered. By night I communed with my own heart,
> and searched my soul.
>
> Psalm 76:6–7

All that follows is what I thought and felt, what life has taught me, what I learned from others with similar mindsets and dispositions. I even dare to say that sometimes the Spirit visited me in the better moments of my life. This book is a part of my very being.

Its contents are not arranged systematically, lest the book lose the immediacy of a diary. So, the thoughts are listed in the order they came to me.

If these fragmentary jottings reveal even a grain of truth, which we are obliged to confess and preach with our actions, our words, and our writings, and if only a few people nurture these grains of truth in their souls, adding to the paucity of my words with their own wisdom, this will serve to be the most treasured reward and the best justification for the publication of this book. This book has no other purpose than to confirm eternal Truth, Good, and Beauty and to magnify the One Who said of Himself: "I am the Way, the Truth, and the Life."

—Archbishop Anastasy, Jerusalem, 1935

Hieromonk Anastasy (Gribanovsky).

PART I

Conversations With My Own Heart
(Thoughts and Musings)

What a divine gift is the word: a gift to command, to captivate, to loose and remit!

Through the word, the Creator has, as it were, deferred to mankind some of His omnipotence.

The word is not merely a symbol of thought; it is a living revelation of our spirit, an incarnation of our reason, the flesh and blood of our emotion, the breath of our will.

In its depths, as in a seed, the pledge of life lies hidden, and if a small seed carries within itself the power to tear cliffs apart, then a living, inspired word can move mountains.

When a word, like a fiery coal, comes out of the crucible of the human spirit, it inspires and inflames thousands of people; it commands even the irrational animals, everywhere revealing its irresistible power. Created long ago by God's almighty Word, the world still trembles at a fiery word of truth, feeling in it a spark of that eternal creative power.

When the Apostle Paul said, "the kingdom of God is not in word but in power" (1 Corinthians 4:20), he did not intend to diminish the significance of the word, for the word itself becomes an instrument of power when it is inspired from above and is truly born of fire and light. Nothing can compare with the word of the incarnate Word, Christ, Who spoke "as one having authority" (Matthew 7:29). The voices of prophets and apostles, anointed from above, declaimed with great power: "Behold, I will cause My words to be fire in your mouth, and this people to be wood, and the fire shall devour them" (Jeremiah 5:14). "The wind [i.e. the Spirit] blows where it wishes …" (John 3:8). "I was but a sheepbreeder and a tender of sycamore fruit," said the Prophet Amos concerning himself. "Then the Lord took me from the sheep, and the Lord said to me, 'Go, prophesy to My people Israel'" (Amos 7:14, 15). And he went—this shepherd of a dumb flock—and began to inflame people's hearts with his word.[1]

As "the word of God is not chained" (2 Timothy 2:9), as it fears no fetters, as it pierces through the walls of prisons, as it vanquishes space and time, as it triumphs over any coercion, so the word of man, insofar as it is a reflection of the divine word and remains true to its purpose, requires an environment of freedom if it is to have any moral authority. Konstantin Aksakov glorifies the ideal of the free word in his hymn:

> Of all God's miracles the height,
> A thought's illumination, flame,
> You are a ray of heavenly light,
> The sigil of humanity's name.
> The lies of ignorance you banish,
> Renewed by endless source of life,
> In your light's truth all dark will vanish,
> O unconstrained word …
> You are the spirit's only sword,
> O unconstrained word.[2]

We all know that talent is a luxury of nature, when the general level is quite middling. But what is talent in its essence? To answer this question is just as difficult as to try to define electricity. We cannot describe its nature, but we feel the presence of this mysterious energy only by how it acts on us and on the world surrounding us. Talent is a scintillating spark of God in a man. It is a calling from above; it is fire and light that warm and illumine our soul. It is the invisible power of God's mercy.

Being aristocratic in nature, talent, like royalty, must initiate its relationship with us. As we approach it, we feel a kind of trepidation, but after we come into contact with it, our heart rejoices as it does on feast days.

Talents, like gems, are valued not only for their magnitude, but for their facets and the way light plays on them.

To turn away from the earthly depths, to rush with an eagle's flight up to the radiant Sun and take others with him—this is the greatest joy, possible for every person on earth. It is, at the same time, the greatest gift that he can give to those around him.

No matter how much people become accustomed to creeping about in the dirt, they will be grateful to anyone who will tear them away from the fallen world and bear them upward to the heavens on powerful wings. People are ready to give everything just for a moment of pure spiritual exhilaration, and they will praise the name of the one who manages to strum the deepest strings of their heart. It is here that we must seek the mystery of the astounding success of Fyodor Dostoyevsky's famous speech at the unveiling of the Pushkin monument in Moscow. The brilliant writer himself later described, in a letter to his wife, the effect of his words on those listening to him:

> I read loudly, with fire. Everything I said about Tatiana was enthusiastically received. When at the end I proclaimed the need for the universal unity of mankind, the audience was ecstatic. When I finished, I will not even tell you of the cries, the roar of elation. People unknown to each other were weeping, crying out, embracing each other, swearing to become better people,

not to hate each other any more, only to love. The order of the assembly broke down: *grande dames*, students, and government bureaucrats were all embracing me, kissing me.

What are we to call this mood of the audience, the very crème de la crème of educated Russian high society, if not a state of spiritual ecstasy, something that, it would seem, our cold intelligentsia is incapable of. With what power the great writer and knower of hearts accomplished this miracle, impelling all of his listeners—with no distinction of age and social status—to feel as brothers and to unite in a single, blessed state of exaltation! He accomplished this, of course, not because of the beautiful style of his delivery (Dostoyevsky was not a particularly polished speaker), but because of the greatness of his proclaimed idea of universal brotherhood, augmented with the fire of exalted inspiration. This was a truly prophetic word that revitalized the hearts of men, forcing them to understand the true meaning of life. Truth made them, if only for a moment, not only free, but elated by their freedom. Here the words of Thomas Carlyle are especially appropriate:

> The great man, with his free force direct out of God's own hand, is lightning. His word is the wise healing word which all can believe in. All blazes round him now, when he has once struck on it, into fire like his own.[3]

Classical antiquity, which developed the art of oratory to the highest level of perfection, left us three major tenets of the art of speaking publicly:

1. The orator must have as his purpose *"docere, delectare, movere,"*[4] that is, he must learn to delight and move (literally, to "incite to movement") simultaneously all three powers of the human soul—the mind, the emotion, and the will.
2. *"Nemo orator, nisi vir bonus,"* said Quintilian. In other words, an evil man can never become a true orator.

3. The speech of an orator must be distinguished by such prosaic clarity that he will not merely be understood, but it would be impossible for him to be misunderstood.

The friends of suffering Job sat speechless at his bier for seven days, and their pensive silence amazes us much more than the subsequent florid speeches pouring out of their mouths in a gushing stream. The most tragic words are usually uttered in a whisper, and when our emotions reach fever pitch, they suppress our ability to speak and force the tongue to cleave to the roof of the mouth. There is nothing more eloquent than death, and death is always wrapped in the mystery of silence.

Alexander Pushkin regretted that to some degree "European affectation and French fastidiousness" had become grafted to the Russian language. He wrote: "I would like the Russian language to always maintain a certain Biblical openness." One can add to this that the directness and spontaneity of Biblical language in no way prevent it from remaining in all ways pure and elevated.

If we ever decide to rewrite our earliest written work, only in the rarest of circumstances will we change the outline of our main ideas, but almost always we find something that requires improvement in style and exposition.

This proves that our thought can never be fully expressed in the form given to it by the word; the thought is always cramped by the Procrustean bed of the word, and our inner sense always finds something not quite expressed, even in our best words. This is why it is so difficult to fit living speech in dead letters, if we want to impart its power in writing.

The farther our inner word travels from its source, the more tangibly it is revealed and given outward form, the more it materializes and coarsens, losing the better part of its spiritual energy, as well as a significant part of its clarity and beauty. Even the most beautiful speech, when rendered in writing, will always lack flesh and blood, an aroma and playfulness of life, with which it captivated people in its original, spoken form. One can reproduce all the phrasing of the orator with literal exactness, but there is no art that allows us to write down the thrill of his inspiration, no camera that can photograph that invisible, spiritual, almost electric charge that pours into the heart of the listener with the sound of his voice, returning back to its source, only to be recharged with new, glittering sparks of his eloquence. Neither can we accurately capture all the accents and musical rhythm of his speech, serving not only as an embellishment, but giving it fullness and finality of expression. In order not to be disillusioned by this dissonance between the living, spoken word and its written form, we prefer to carry the word that so moved us, like a beautiful melody, in our hearts, rather than to see its soulless reflection in corpse-dead letters. To our joy, a human word spoken aloud to the world never dies, but, like a crystallized part of our spirit, survives unto eternity.

No matter how much we strive to be original, inadvertently we often repeat ourselves. There is nothing unnatural in this. Our thought, like a horse, wanders without thinking back to a familiar road. The entire history of mankind moves along well-trod paths.

Theoretical and practical talents rarely coincide in one and the same person. There are people who think like geniuses, and people who act like foolish children.

A painting has to be looked at in proper perspective. Similarly, the quality of any of our own creative work can only be assessed after the passage of time. We have to wait until it separates from our immediate perception—with which it becomes interwoven in the process of its creation—and becomes for us object conducive to external scrutiny.

Brilliant people, that is, geniuses, are merely a focal point for the creative energy of an entire epoch. Therefore, it is not surprising that they often define their respective epoch in human history.

Hamlets are not created to rule the world; however, they are indispensable for the world as moral foils and accusing consciences.

A wise man or a scientist has the same moral responsibility toward other people as a rich man has to the poor. Fortunate is he who can say, together with Solomon, "So I learned both honestly and ungrudgingly, and I do not hide her [wisdom's] wealth" (Wisdom of Solomon 7:13).

Sometimes our soul is dead and dry as a desert; at other times it is on fire with such creative energy that our heart trembles from the profusion of thoughts and emotions, and the weak vessel of our body can hardly bear the pressure of our boiling inner state.

Even the brightest idea, when thrown into the mass of humanity, quickly becomes worn, murky, and flat, like a coin that has been long in circulation, constantly passed from hand to hand.

It has been known even from the deepest antiquity that the truth is by no means always on the side of the majority. "You shall not follow a crowd to do evil," Moses said to Israel, "nor join with them, so as to turn aside with the majority to pervert justice" (Exodus 23:2).

"When the Saviour was born in the world, the oxen calmly munched on hay," said Heinrich Heine. You who read, pay attention! Because, of course, the sardonic poet is not accusing the irrational animals.

A fully ripened thought strives of itself toward the light of God's world in the same way as a chick pecks its way out of the egg when the time is right.

There exists a general opinion that only misfortunes bring people to God, while happiness has a tendency to tie them to the world, and forces them to forget Him. However, there are exceptions to this rule. Nikolay Pirogov writes in his autobiography that the first days of his married life were full of such blessedness that his soul seemed to melt and become purified, and he, although previously ailing with unbelief, came to see God in the effulgence of his marital bliss.

In the very moment that the woman with an issue of blood secretly touched the robes of Christ the Saviour and received healing from Him, He felt the power coming out of Him. Every person has a similar sensation when he wants to transfer his life force into another creature, like unto himself.

The mother giving birth to her child on her bed of pain feels this force leaving her. Anyone who becomes one in heart with a suffering neighbor feels the same, because he has, as it were, become "reincarnated" as his suffering neighbor. Any teacher or preacher of the truth sacrifices the same life-force when his words become alight with the fires of inspiration. In his every word, he gives his listeners, as it were, a transfusion from his own heart, and as he lights the fire in others, he inevitably fades himself.

A person can seem both great and insignificant, depending on the perspective of the viewer—from below, that is, comparing him to other earthly creatures, or from above, that is, from the height of absolute divine perfection.

Whoever tries to keep up with the times will die together with them. General popularity flatters our vanity, but it is no pledge of our immortality. He who lives on in the memory is one who warns of coming times. Often, he lives alone and is misunderstood by his contemporaries.

Many people seem to be brilliant from a distance, blinding others with their blazing talents. But as soon as you approach them, you become convinced that they are gilded, not truly gold. Everything with them is on the surface, under which we seek in vain for deposits of genuine spiritual values.

One can say the same thing about a person and the sun: both are better seen during the setting than during the rising.

The brightest stars in the firmament of history often appear unexpectedly. "A great man has no need of ancestors," said one of these bright stars (Frederick the Great).

With equal fairness, we can say that such a person leaves no direct descendants, for genius usually is not passed on to one's children.

Rather, one can even say the opposite: spiritual riches that have fallen on the lot of a chosen one of Providence are dissipated in a single generation, and even their poor remnants are not always passed on.

Fathers, in spite of their own wishes, end up luxuriating at the expense of their children, leaving them often entirely dispossessed.

In our life's journey, we often meet people who, according to the French proverb, age badly with long acquaintance. The longer we weigh them, the more we realize they are quite empty. However, there are others whom we do not even notice at first, and only later do they reveal the depths of their inner life.

Whoever cannot guard his tongue imperceptibly wastes his store of spiritual energy with every idle word. Not by accident, a certain ascetic compared a babbler to a steam room with its doors left open, allowing all the steam to escape. Restraint in speech helps us to conserve our inner strength, which when it needs can flow out with great power, turning our speech into a stream of fire.

David's "heart grew hot within [him], and while [he] was thus musing, the fire kindled." This occurred when he "was mute and held [his] peace," when he "kept silent, even from good words" (Psalm 38:3–4).

The tongue of Zacharias, when loosed from his muteness, uttered a stream of inspired prophecy.

"I am full of words," explained the youngest of Job's friends, Elihu, when it was his turn to speak. "Indeed, my stomach is like a wineskin of sweet new wine, bound up and ready to burst ... I will speak, that I may find relief in opening my lips" (Job 32:18–20). I will speak and be relieved—who has not experienced such a state, when the soul, like a cloud full to bursting with moisture, rains down a torrent of words and through this is relieved?

Our earth-bound perspective is so limited that often "no one can say, 'What is this? Why is that?'" (Wisdom of Sirach 39:21). But "everything will be revealed in its due time," the wise Sirach consoles us.[5]

Friedrich Schiller was the first to express the following undisputed truth, Leo Tolstoy after him: "In order to do something great, you have to concentrate all the powers of your soul into a single point."

People are ready to debase themselves to any condition, except to be ridiculed. They hardly ever forgive anyone for making them look ridiculous. Woe to him who even once in his life finds himself in a similar situation.

It would be fair to call our mind a slave both lazy and false. It rarely takes the time to develop a serious thought to its conclusion, always looking for a way to shorten its work and come up with a quick and easy solution, even if it is the wrong one. Furthermore, it easily sells its birthright to the passions and hidden desires, as though bribed by them. It is no wonder that the ancients used to say, "*Non persuader noleutem*," that is, don't try to convince someone who has no desire to be convinced.

At the same time, the will is the father of reason. When our mind abdicates its self-rule in favor of emotion and will, it loses just as much as if—in the blindness of pride—it appropriates to itself infallibility, even in matters that are strictly regulated. In the same way as one can have a depraved heart, one can also have a depraved manner of thinking, with a darkened inner light. As strange as this may seem, there are some people who willingly want to be fooled; this occurs because truth always places one under obligation, and so they fear to look truth in the face. The building blocks of falsehood are often faint-heartedness and cowardice. In general, fruitful work of the mind requires moral labor (*ascesis*), and only pure hearts can see the face of Eternal Truth.

Every person is given his own unique spiritual abilities, which he cannot widen even if he wishes it. Therefore, one must not demand from another more than he is able to accomplish according to the limitations of his own nature. It is useless to search for the music of those strings that do not resonate in his heart.

A fiery spirit eventually burns up its fleshly vessel, just as a sword eventually wears down its scabbard.

"To the pure all things are pure, but to those who are defiled and unbelieving nothing is pure; but even their mind and conscience are defiled" (Titus 1:15).

There are people who can be compared to a twisted mirror: in their perception the entire world looks perverted.

True eloquence is not defined merely by simplicity and elegance of speech. Even the most refined phrases soon begin to grate on the ear, like a repeated drumbeat, if they are hollow on the inside. However, words that are filled with healthy, serious thought and decorated with genuine feeling demand our attention, even when the speaker is obviously laboring through an unpolished speech. Perfect public speaking is only attained when there is a perfect harmony between content and external form, when they merge into such a monolith that the two can no longer be separated. The smallest breakdown in this harmony weakens the power and quality of the words spoken. Although Tolstoy said, "a cropped style dries out the thought," that doesn't mean that the thought should be raw, unrefined matter encased in a cover of randomly chosen words. Mastery of classical style always means purity and graceful perfection. Like a well-fitted suit, the word must gracefully complement the thought, without limiting its free and supple movement. At the same time, the word must be like a golden coin that has not only its own brilliance and form, but a certain weight that gives it corresponding worth.

The entire sun is sometimes reflected in a single, small drop of water. In the same way, sometimes the entire person is visible in a single expression, or even in a single word.

"Even so the tongue is a little member and boasts great things … For every kind of beast and bird, of reptile and creature of the sea, is tamed and has been tamed by mankind. But no man can tame the tongue. It is an unruly evil …" (James 3:5–8).

Apostolic utterance was needed to give such powerful expression to the harm that a tongue inflicts on its owner, if he loses his authority over it. The greatest of goods then becomes the worst and unruliest of evils, striving to rule over us.

The decadent periods of all civilizations, especially the twilight of Classical Greco-Roman culture, are remarkable simultaneously for a hollowing out of the human soul and hypertrophy of the word, which turns from a means to an end in itself.

During such times, an orator becomes nothing more than a professional, and not only he but even the prophets have a lie "in their mouth, and their heart pursues their own [gain]" (Ezekiel 33:29 (LXX)).

The orator of such times truckles to a morally degenerating society with unworthy wordplay—not innocent wordplay, which can serve to decorate elaborate speech, but criminal misuse of language, when not words but the ideas indicated by them are played with and switched back and forth in disingenuous sophistry, thanks to which truth and virtue are ridiculed, while lies and vice are justified. All together, this leads to intellectual and moral chaos, a poison that Mephistopheles—that father of lies and true ancestor of all sophistry—tries to instill in his naive student in this very illuminating and characteristic dialogue from Johann von Goethe's *Faust*:

Mephistopheles
On *words* let your attention centre!
Through the safest gate you'll enter
The temple-halls of Certainty.
Student
Yet in the word must some idea be.
Mephistopheles
Of course! But only shun too over-sharp a tension,
For just where fails the comprehension,
A word stops promptly in as deputy.
With words 'tis excellent disputing;
Systems to words 'tis easy suiting;
On words 'tis excellent believing;
No word can ever lose a jot from thieving.[6]

Such twisting of the word is characteristic of our own times, which have given rise to so many professional "talking heads" and sophists. The less capable these people are of doing anything serious, the more they appear to be the windbags that they are, getting drunk on their own empty loquacity. What is the word, then, except an "empty sound," with no more value than greenbacks hurled in excess into circulation.[7] Like money, words have now lost their previous worth, not having the gold standard to back them up, that is, real, substantial content and strength of will. Our great Russia is drowning in a flood of words, and from the roiling waters of untrammeled idle talk Leviathan the dragon has reared his head. This is the price we have paid for becoming enamored of the fruitless fig tree of the word; and yet, all the spiritual leaders and standard-bearers of our times are groaning with labor pains just to utter some new, previously unheard, miraculous word for the anxiously awaiting world. What a pointless exercise! They will give us nothing new, only proving Ivan Bunin's immortal words:

> I learned how useless and worn-out
> The hollow word of man can be.[8]

Enough useless speeches! We are satiated with them, and they will soon make us feel aversion to the most noble of all human gifts. We need not orators, but inspired prophets, laborers of duty, and creators of a new life.

We would not be so often mistaken in people if we expected mediocrity or weakness, instead of expecting every person we meet to be a hero of the spirit, of whom there are so few on this earth. Idealizing others is an attribute of youth. Having become accustomed to measuring everyone by its own lofty strivings, youth must often pay for such naiveté with bitter disillusionment.

A certain master orator greeted every new beautiful or ingenious turn of phrase with such envy that he always said, "I am sorry that it was not I who said it."

Great ideas, when absorbed into the flesh and blood of humanity, become part of the everyday reality of our life, and through this they lose their initial originality and brilliance. However, this should not diminish their value, nor should those who first uttered the great idea lose their deserved praise. Therefore, we should always remember them with a sense of reverent gratitude.

"Laurels do not grow for the lazy man," said Frederick the Great. It would be a serious mistake to think that the most remarkable scientific discoveries or the greatest works of philosophy or the arts are accomplished without any effort of will, or only in a surge of inspiration. Thomas Edison famously rejected this incorrect opinion with the sincere admission that in his great discoveries, 99% was perspiration and only 1% was inspiration. Buffon was no less emphatic in his words: "Half of genius is hard work." Pushkin also confirmed this in his actions, covering his manuscripts with many corrections and rewrites. No talent is free from the necessity of hard work, which was established as a requirement for mankind after the expulsion from Eden. Every gift is only an opportunity or a seed that must then be watered with sweat and tears, and sometimes even blood, if one is to bear worthy fruit.

The brilliant Franz Liszt quite accurately noted that only a "half-talent" can be taught, because true genius teaches itself. This does not mean, however, that the genius does not depend on his predecessors or his environment, from which he received his spiritual nourishment, as a plant is nourished by soil. If a genius were separated from the world in early childhood and left to his own devices, his imagination would create no more than childhood fantasies, and he would vainly tire himself in attempts to create something great. Only God can create out of nothing.

"I would have written more briefly to you if I had more time." These paradoxical words of Voltaire are in large part true. Verbosity is almost always a sign of hurrying or not thinking through a subject. Sometimes a great deal of effort must be expended in order to distill a thought so that, like a plant extract, it can give a great deal in a small amount.

When we worry, our soul, like the sea, dredges up to the surface all that usually hides at the bottom of our heart.

There are thoughts bright as the summer sun, weighty as a ripe stalk of wheat, clearly defined by a powerful chisel on all sides like something wrought out of iron and steel. Then there are thoughts dim as an autumn day, nebulous, loose, and colorless as dough, something like twilight or dense fog in which there is no definite shape, no clarity, no brilliance, no power, no beauty.

Sometimes, we don't merely suffer "woe from wit,"[9] but gain wits from woe, if only the sorrow doesn't crush us under its weight.

A bright and calm state of the spirit usually serves as the most fruitful soil for creative work, but sometimes inspiration comes in the form of thunder and storm clouds. From the dark clouds that obscure the horizon of our soul, bright flashes of lighting begin to illuminate the far reaches.

A thought that breaks through an obstacle standing in its way gathers twice the energy and, like a waterfall, rushes forward inexorably. The soul, shaken to its depths by the experience, is like a well-tilled field covered with fresh, fertile loam, in which new ideas can be planted and grown.

"How long, you simple ones, will you love simplicity? For scorners delight in their scorning, And fools hate knowledge." (Proverbs 1:22 (NKJV))

These questions could only come from the lips of a wise man: they do not exist for the ignorant and the fool, no more than light exists for the blind men. The greatest misfortune for these people is that they do not recognize their spiritual poverty and do not want to buy purified gold for their enrichment.

To destroy one of our passions using another passion is the same thing as allowing one kind of harmful bacteria to grow in your body at the expense of another, even though the former is more likely to kill you.

There is a law of spiritual inheritance, a kind of spiritual chain reaction: when we come into contact with a great thought or exalted state, within us immediately arise a series of reflected thoughts and exalted emotions and desires. For this reason alone we should strive to commune with great teachers and spiritual leaders of mankind, to delve deeply into the study of their lives and works, which are an image of their spirit.

St Basil the Great and St Gregory the Theologian were united by a close friendship, and during their school years in Athens, they avoided the company of their other friends, knowing that it is easier to catch someone else's disease than to pass on one's own healthy state.

Tolstoy confessed that he rewrote some of his own works too many times, to their own detriment. From this it is evident that there is a limit to "turning over the stylus."[10] If he goes too far, the writer wastes the keenness of his inner sense that determines the limits of what is more or less perfect in his literary work. Here we see the obvious truth of a general psychological principle: familiarity with a given object dulls our receptivity and interest, and can even lead to a temporary spiritual apathy toward that object.

"Be brief; say much in a few words," says Sirach to the young man. "Act like a man who knows, yet holds his tongue" (Wisdom of Sirach 32:8–9). It would be well if not only young people kept to this rule. Far from all people in mature years know how to be moderate in language, in order to say no more and no less that necessary for a given purpose. "They do not know how to speak, but neither do they know how to be silent," according to an ancient Roman proverb. It is interesting that those who have the greatest gifts of eloquence are often the most moderate in speech. Metropolitan Philaret—that treasury of the mind and word who raised an entire generation of brilliant teachers—was such a man. "Do not say much," he told his listeners in one of his homilies, "even though you are capable of saying many good things. Under no circumstances should you recklessly waste words, the creation of the word, the creative word."

"How often did I regret it when I spoke, but never when I remained silent," said St Arsenios the Great.

The ancient wise man, having carefully observed the fate of mankind on earth, left us, among others, the following life lesson: "Before its destruction, the heart of a man exalts itself, and before its glory, it humbles itself" (Proverbs 18:12).

There is the outer word that merely exits the lips—this is a "sounding brass or a clanging cymbal" (1 Corinthians 13:1). It will not master our soul, even if it falls in cascades and with the noise and spume of a waterfall. Then there is the inner word, born in the depths of our being, comprising the breath of our creative spirit and bearing its fiery stamp. These words are "powers," as Fr Paul Florensky once named them so evocatively. They overwhelm the human heart and direct the movement of the world. Mephistopheles in Goethe's *Faust* accurately defined the essential difference between the two:

> But ne'er from heart to heart you'll speak inspiring,
> Save your own heart is eloquent![11]

The mouth speak with authority only when the heart is full, but since the heart can contain either good or evil, then the word filled with spiritual energy can bear within itself the seed of either good or evil. Truly "life and death are in the hand of a tongue" (Proverbs 18:21).

Immeasurable is the abyss separating the spirit-bearing words of the Apostles, the great teachers, and ascetics of the Church from the putrid and often blasphemous words of the communists, bringing forth evil from their corrupt hearts. The evil caused by their propaganda is beyond all description. Their speech is "a way of speaking comparable to death" (Wisdom of Sirach 23:12), spreading like cancer. Their "tongue is a fire, a world of iniquity ... full of deadly poison" (James 3: 6–8).

Borne on radio waves, their vile words, poisoned by lies and hatred, spread over the whole world, combine with other such words and concepts and, becoming one with the consciousness of a society, will be absorbed even into the flesh and blood of mankind, where the poison will continue its noxious work for a long time. Sins of the word have no statue of limitations; therefore, the perpetrator who misuses this greatest of gifts is far more culpable even than a thief or a robber, as the famous fable teaches us.[12]

After intense mental exercise, our mind remains in movement for a long time simply by inertia, reminding one of the continuing unrest of the waves after an already calmed storm, or the continuing turning of a wheel after the drive belt has been taken off.

There is a tyranny of love, and a tyranny of habit. Both tyrannies are equally vehement, both depriving us of our freedom.

One must have a strong and truly exalted spirit in order to bear the weight of honor, power, and glory without falling spiritually ill. Weak souls cannot bear such testing, and they are crushed under the weight of temptation.

A person is not always equal to himself; sometimes he rises above himself, but more often he falls below his normal level.

Vissarion Belinsky accurately defined Pushkin's "multi-dimensionality" when he said, "Even the simplest emotion resounds with all possible strings and therefore is never monotonous, being instead always a perfectly harmonious chord." Pushkin considered himself to be a "universal man,"[13] and compared himself to an echo, reflecting in himself every sound in the world. The echo then finds its "retro-reflection" in the soul of the reader who recognized himself in the writings of the genius-poet. "But these are my own wishes and thought," we say to ourselves with wonder. "The poet has uttered that which I myself thought. I would have wanted to say the same!"

The most dangerous approach to public speaking is one where the person does not rule over his words, but his words rule over him, when the word rushes ahead of the thought, not remaining in line with the flow of thoughts. Such a temperament in oratory can lead a speaker farther than he wishes and abandon him at a shameful dead end, from which he can find no exit.

In the same way that a talented musician can produce the most diverse sounds from a single instrument, an experienced orator has the ability to strum on all the strings of the human heart at once. Pushkin's description of Rossini's music can also apply to the orator:

He pours out fluid harmonies,
They boil, they flow, they burn,[14]

He can thunder, he can storm, he can scorch his hearers like lightning, or he can plunge like a two-edged sword into their very marrow, into the depths of their hearts, tearing them to bits. Sometimes his speech burbles quietly and comfortingly like a brook, or it caresses the ear like a panpipe. Sometimes he can inspire passionate enthusiasm, sometimes he can confuse, disturb, and even horrify, and all this is only so that the words that follow will be like a healing balsam on the perturbed soul of the listener. The final chords of his speech are usually bright and exhilarating and only in rare cases, when the hearer needs to be especially impressed, does the last chord sound in a tragic minor, through which, however, a ray of sun still shines. Unclear notes and unresolved dissonances are just as inappropriate at the end of a speech as at the end of a musical composition.

The word has its own system of ethics that requires it to be pure, honorable, and chaste. Wherever this rule is not followed, wherever the tongue is a plaything of the passions and sudden moods, wherever the word is bought and sold or just a frivolous matter for sport, there begins the adultery of the word, that is, betrayal of its pure and exalted calling. It is not by accident that G.K. Chesterton included the following phrase in his famous hymn:

> From lies of tongue and pen,
> From all the easy speeches
> That comfort cruel men
> Deliver us, good Lord.[15]

Into every person, the Creator laid down a reserve of potential energy that usually only shows itself in the most important or challenging moments of our lives. Only thus can one explain why a mediocre, apparently in no way remarkable, person suddenly grows into a true hero filled with might in moments of danger or when fulfilling an important mission unexpectedly assigned to him.

Exalted truths and genuine beauty always appear to us simple and clear as a ray of the sun. But this simplicity is only apparent: if you pass a sun's ray through a prism, you will see that it is a harmonious fusion of the seven colors of the visible spectrum, each one of which remains invisible on its own to our eyes.

If the Classical style captivates us with the purity and beauty of its lines, this only occurs because everywhere there is observed a strict proportionality of all parts, established by a strict mathematical ratio. The simplest of truths usually occurs to us last of all, because it is the result of long preceding mental work.

They say that orators are not born, but made. This assertion is inherently incorrect. Everyone knows that some have a special, natural gift of speaking, but it must be assiduously cultivated and constantly practiced to be developed fully. When Demosthenes was already in the full bloom of his rhetorical glory, his enemies used to say that his speeches "stank of the night lantern." This is how carefully he polished his speeches, and only thanks to this do they still glisten today, remaining unsurpassed in their power and sweet-smelling beauty.

People often try to combine genius with holiness, as "two phenomena" that, according to one thinker, "go beyond the boundaries of canonical norms of culture."[16] Their affinity is revealed thus: a genius is often inspired in a way that Plato called "divine inspiration." This is the true breath of divinity in a person, which gives gifts to people wherever and as much as It wishes. The ancient pagan philosophers, poets, and artists, beginning with Socrates and Phidias, vividly felt the presence of some kind of higher power that illumined them in moments of creative work. It was not by accident that Phidias, in almost pious compunction, fell on his face before one his best sculptures. The same sense of presence has also been felt by other gifted people of the modern age. "A genius is naive," said Schiller, "because his thoughts are of divine origin."[17] Goethe elaborates a similar idea in his famous letter to Eckermann. Gabriel Séailles, a French religious philosopher of the late nineteenth century, wrote that genius is a gift of grace whose work is like a prayer heard by god. But perhaps no one suffered this touch of heavenly fire in his soul as deeply as did Pushkin. He always clearly distinguished himself from his muse, even comparing the calling of a poet to that of a prophet by calling him a "divine messenger." The revert awe experienced by the great poet in moments of inspiration is unwillingly passed on to his readers, and this, perhaps, is the clearest proof of his true genius.

In order for a mind to seem brilliant to the corrupted tastes of our modern society, its sharp edge should always be poisoned with skepticism and acerbic criticism. Positive minds, no matter how great their dignity, always seem dim or mawkish to such people, even though these minds create the spiritual and artistic culture of the world.

Sometimes there is noise without glory, but glory never comes unaccompanied by noise. This noise can truly exhaust people if they live a constant holiday that never alternates with a simple weekday.

"I am afraid of glory," recently said one of these chosen ones of glory, and his words were, of course, sincere. Every heady pleasure of glory has the ability to depress our soul and even our consciousness to some degree at its most intense moment. It is like a pleasant, but intense, dream or the state of slight intoxication, when one's head begins to spin. We can enjoy glory much more meaningfully in memory, when we are freed from the immediate power of its captivating emotions, which Pushkin himself called a "sweet illness."

The nation, that collective organism, is just as prone to deifying itself as the individual person. The madness of pride here grows as exponentially as any passion that catches fire in a society, refracted among thousands and millions of souls.

"Everything great is accomplished in an inspiration of love or with strong religious feelings," said Mussolini.[18] However, in essence these two phenomena always coincide with each other. True love is fed by true religion, just as true religion is inseparable from love.

Arthur Schopenhauer wondered, "that a means like rhythm or rhyme, seeming so trivial, nay, childish, should exercise such an effect, is very striking and well worth investigation." He explains this effect by the fact that the music of poetry caresses our ear of itself; when we add to the music of poetry a brilliant thought, it appears to us as an unexpected gift, "like the words to music."[19] This explanation of Schopenhauer, however, is probably more witty than actually true. In actual fact, here we must see the action of the same law by which a beautiful painting is given added effect by being put in an appropriate frame. People everywhere search for the manifestations of the ideal of the trinity-in-unity of truth, goodness, and beauty, and pay special attention whenever the true is married to the beautiful. Speaking of poetry in general, its music organically harmonizes with thought, as Carlyle explained beautifully. He found no other way of calling it than "musical thought":

> A *musical* thought is one spoken by a mind that has penetrated into the inmost heart of the thing; detected the inmost mystery

of it, namely the melody that lies hidden in it; the inward harmony of coherence which is the its soul, whereby it exists, and
has a right to be, here in this world … The Poet is he who *thinks*
in that manner [in a musical way] … See deep enough, and you
will see musically; the heart of Nature *being* everywhere music,
if you can only reach it.[20]

It is remarkable that all of us complain of the heaviness of life's yoke.
However, the longer we live on this earth, the more we root deep into
it like a tree. In mature and even old age, a person has a much harder
time parting with this earthly vale than in youth. In the spring of life,
when life foams and pours over the edge like young wine, a person
is ready every minute to shake the dust off his feet, to take wing, and
fly like a fleet-winged bird. Then, these words of the poet are most
familiar to our soul:

> And long did the soul on this earth find no calm,
> With wondrous desires replete.
> And melodies earthly provided no balm,
> So longed she for heavenly psalms.[21]

Theoretical rejection of religion is often merely an excuse for personal apathy toward religious faith, and it often comes from a desire
to lull the conscience, which punishes a person for his sinful life. The
so-called free thinker strives not so much to preserve an ability to
think independently—faith can get along quite well with independent thinking, as we see with many illustrious scientists and thinkers—
rather, he only really wants the liberty to follow the dictates of his own
heart and will, and to free himself from those moral obligations and
limitations that religion inevitably prescribes for us. Blaise Pascal was
fully justified to suspect the honor and sincerity of people who try not
to think about God and man's calling, and who do not even want to

conscientiously investigate what they so frivolously reject. "Nothing," he said, "reveals more an extreme weakness of mind than not to know the misery of a godless man … Nothing is more dastardly than to act with bravado before God."²²

"I would like to believe," some say, "but I cannot."

"No," you should answer them, "you can believe, but you do not wish to."

The source of the precious treasure of faith is first of all in your own heart. Hear the witness of your own conscience, listen to the voice that comes from your immortal spirit, search for faith, and you will find it. God Himself will open the door closed before you, if only you knock insistently. He knows the weakness of our nature, and he requires of us faith at least as small as a grain of mustard seed. "If you can believe," Christ said to the unfortunate father of the possessed youth at the foot of Tabor, "all things are possible to him who believes." "Lord, I believe; help my unbelief!" (Mark 9:23–24). This was the answer, or rather the tearful prayer of the father, and this was enough. The miracle was accomplished. Every person must pray with the same words in moments of spiritual temptation, for all of us have surges of faith, followed by an ebb tide, as one eminent bishop-theologian said. When faith raises us up on its mighty waves, our spirit expands, as it were, feeling unconquerable inner firmness and strength truly capable of moving mountains. One cannot help but be spiritually inspired when reading the majestic words of the Apostle Paul concerning the great men of the Old Testament, who "through faith subdued kingdoms, worked righteousness… stopped the mouths of lions … became valiant in battle" (Hebrews 11:33–34). Without faith there are no heroes of the spirit, as there is no true creativity. A man "with no dogma," whom Henrik Senkevich described so vividly, always inspires pity in us. He is a reed shaken by the wind, a spiritual paralytic, incapable of moving from one place to another, even if he is gifted with genius. The doubter is truly "like a wave of the sea driven and tossed by the wind … he is a double-minded man, unstable in all his ways" (James 1:6–8).

Once I entered a prison cell where two men condemned to death were sitting. With no little fear I crossed the threshold of this ill-fated room, seeming to me no better than an open grave. I was afraid I would not be able to find the necessary words to comfort and encourage these unfortunate men. How great was my amazement when I found them nonchalantly boiling tea over a kerosene lamp; they apparently thought that the few days separating them from execution were still enough time for them to put off thinking about death and to enjoy life. This is man: he always walks on the edge of the abyss, in ever-present danger of falling, but like an imprudent child he continues to frivolously pick the flower hanging over the edge. "Between us and heaven or hell there is only life," said Pascal, "which is the frailest thing in the world. We run carelessly to the precipice, after we have put something before us to prevent us seeing it."[23]

No one wants to leave this world without leaving some trace of himself. Every person strives to leave an inheritance to the coming ages and to create for himself a monument on this earth, built by hands or not. The mere thought that an idea that we embed into our creation will outlive us, that this idea will give life and inspiration to many generations to come, that it will bring many unknown people to us, who will bless our name—this has always captivated man. However, this completely natural feeling—doubtless an echo of our thirst for immortality—is sometimes combined with a hidden spirit of vainglory, which follows our heels like a shadow. Even the very etymology of the word shows the uselessness of following after glory.[24] However, such a feeling is perhaps the most powerful spring that impels mankind's creative energy.

How many people waste all their strength in various efforts only to sparkle for a moment, like a meteor on the horizon, attracting the attention of the whole world! Others are even willing to give their very life for a moment of evanescent glory. Literary vainglory is all but the most dangerous and infectious of these kinds of feelings. Who does not secretly dream of the time when he will rule over other minds or with a mighty hand strum the strings of another's heart? Even the rulers of nations are not free from these human weaknesses. Many of them, not content with the role of benefactor and the high honors resulting from their exalted position, would have liked to cover their shining crowns with the humble laurels of the poet, the writer, the artist.

Tolstoy said of his own elder brother that he was no less a literary talent than himself, but he did not become a great writer only because he did not have a writer's "usual weaknesses" (to quote Turgenev), including the most important one—vainglory. At the same time, admitted Tolstoy with his typical sincerity, he himself could never remain indifferent to his own glory and the opinion of society regarding his works.

With the same captivating power of sincerity, Pascal writes about the temptation of vainglory:

> Vanity [vainglory] is so anchored in the heart of man that a soldier, a soldier's servant, a cook, a porter brags, and wishes to have his admirers. Even philosophers wish for them. Those who write against it want to have the glory of having written well; and those who read it desire the glory of having read it. I who write this have perhaps this desire, and perhaps those who will read it.[25]

It is remarkable that people are capable of taking pride in anything, not only in glory, but in the lack of glory, not only in beauty, but in ugliness as well, not only in virtue, but in vice as well. Finally, people are capable of being proud of their humility, which in essence is the rejection of pride and victory over it. Incontestable is the word of St John of the Ladder: "No matter how you throw this pitchfork, it always lands with the sharp end pointing upward."[26]

There is a special type of person who appears to be not of this world even from his childhood. He is too bright and pure to long remain on this earth, lest he becomes fouled with its dirt. He walks over the face of the earth like a phantom, barely touching the ground with his feet, and he flies away to eternity usually at a young age, leaving behind him universal regret at his passing.

The wise Solomon speaks of such people when he remembers God taking Enoch before his time, "lest evil change his understanding or deceit deceive his soul…. For in a short time he fulfilled long years" (Wisdom of Solomon 4:11, 13).

Hegel (Georg Wilhelm Friedrich) said that it is not chains that make a slave, but the self-consciousness that he is a slave. If this is so, then one can feel free even when bound in chains.

We often encounter a mind that sparkles with a steely, cold kind of shine. It illumines, but does not warm, like a winter sun. It is not strange that such a mind repels our soul more often than it attracts, since our soul searches for light and warmth together in a mind.

Hard work was created for every man and a heavy yoke for the sons of Adam, from the day they come forth from their mother's womb until the day they return to the mother of all. The conception of things to come and the day of death trouble their thoughts and cause fear of heart—from the one sitting on a glorious throne to the one humbled in earth and ashes, from the one wearing purple and a crown to the one clothed in burlap, there is anger, envy, trouble, and unrest, and fear of death and fury and strife. When it is time for rest on his bed, his night of sleep alters his knowledge. (Wisdom of Sirach 40:1–5)

This is the sorrowful lot of all mortals who live on this earth. In spite of this, they hold on to life as it slips away with a shuddering hand, desiring to lengthen it even for a few more seconds.

"Let a man meet a bear robbed of her cubs, rather than a fool in his folly" (Proverbs 17:12 (NKJV)). A fool can be more dangerous than an angry mother bear, evidently only because we cannot anticipate from where and when he will choose to attack us.

"*Partir c'est mourir un peu*," say the French (To part is to die a little bit). We feel this every time we leave our home country or the people who are dear to us. Sorrow is inescapably intertwined with every parting, especially if the parting is for a long time or forever.

It is an interesting fact that great writers are almost never born in small countries. There seems to be a lack of air and expanse of horizon, and great writers need to be brought up in an atmosphere of universal, all-encompassing human culture, which is hard to find in small nations with their narrow nationalism and provincial culture.

The essence of power is will. The same root is used in many languages (Latin: *potestas*, French: *puissance*, English: power, even the German *könig*), and all of them indicate capacity for power. Weak power (often the most cruel, because it leaves behind itself many unnecessary casualties) slips easily from the grasp of those who wield it, and then others take it up, others with more strength, although these regents and usurpers may have a less gentle hand. Society will always follow a fanatic or charismatic maverick before they follow a great-hearted dreamer who has no ability to turn word into action.

The Philosopher-kings of Plato's ideal society would probably have been quite pathetic in this sense, and would have inevitably wrecked the ship of state. A firm, yet at the same time enlightened, reasonable, and responsible authority must be the desire of every country, but such good fortune is rarely the lot of nations and governments.

"Assessing someone and condemning are close."[27] Beginning with the first, we unnoticeably fall into the second.

Many historically great men experience the flowering of their glory in the time when "genius and fortune, still young and virginal, carry them forward as though on two gentle wings," so that their fame does not darken the purity of their hearts. But as soon as they become aware of their success, their sun begins to set.

Christianity brought with it a completely self-sufficient spiritual world order that is firmly established on its own foundation. The leaven of the Gospel, once it had entered mankind, should not have been mixed with the "old leaven" of the spirit of this world, which deeply penetrates the heart of the personal and social life of mankind and becomes like a second nature. The Kingdom of Christ, from the first day of its establishment on this earth, placed itself in opposition to the world as separate from it and even antagonistic to its first principles. The science of Christian moral perfection is found in a series of antinomies resulting from this opposition. Thus, for example, one must humble oneself to be raised up. One must be weak to become strong. One must become a fool to attain true wisdom. One must reject everything to obtain everything. One must lay down one's life to receive it once more. One must die in order to resurrect and live eternally. Here we see an obvious contrast of two mutually exclusive orders and principles of life, between which there can be no permanent—or even temporary—alliance. One must pass away for the other to flourish on its ruins. Any attempt to throw a bridge between them has always led to a secularization of Christianity and to a lowering of its exalted ideal.

A person can sometimes speak with equal facility in several languages, but his own language will be the only one in which he thinks.

"It is as though you did not leave Me, but yourselves," said the Lord to His unfaithful, rebellious son Israel.[28] Having rejected God, Who is the Source of light and joy, in Whom our very personhood receives its deepest confirmation, we truly betray our own selves, reject what is our highest good, kill our best inclinations, bury our brightest hopes, and waste the only true meaning and bulwark for our life.

"Did not our heart burn within us while He talked with us on the road ... ?" (Luke 24:32).

The heart of man is always on fire when Truth converses with it. Whoever has not experienced this does not know Truth.

It is remarkable that in childhood and youth we often want to be—or at least appear to be—older than our years, but in the second half of our lives we begin to sigh over our lost youth. In this way, we seem to want to unite the advantages of both periods of our life, to fill out the gaps in each, as in the famous French axiom: "O, if only old age could do everything! O, if only youth could know everything!"

However, God has arranged it in such a way that one generation always needs the other, thereby more tightly binding people of different ages. Vigorous, but often nearsighted, youth carries on its shoulders tired, but far-seeing old age, so that the elder can show the sure road through life to the younger. Wherever this union between the old and the young generations is ruptured, a path is blazed to general catastrophe.

The famous Russian proverb "the morning is wiser than the evening" is taken, of course, from the treasury of many centuries of human experience.

But it is also fully supported by findings in psychology. In the morning, after our nervous system has been refreshed by sleep, the light of our consciousness burns especially brightly. However, our consciousness does not stop working even while we sleep, preparing a solution to this or this question. In the morning hours, the question takes center stage in our perception, unobstructed by other impressions, and our mind exerts all its energy to its solution. As a result, the object that seemed so dark and unclear to us the previous night immediately brightens with the light of day. I know of many cases when the solution to complicated mathematical formulas and even important scientific breakthroughs were worked out during sleep.

"England expects that every man will do his duty." In this signal sent by Admiral Nelson before the Battle of Trafalgar, the English character reveals itself completely. If we add their native conservatism and their so-called common sense, which never leaves an Englishman even in moments of intense stress, it becomes obvious why they are an especially vigorous and stable nation.

Only shallow tides make a lot of noise. Deep waters flow calmly. We often see a reflection of this natural order in the psychological makeup of people.

The substance of great writers' contributions to the world of *belles lettres* is usually limited to a few original thoughts. The rest is merely elaboration and explanation, or even repetition, of the same essential themes of their creative thought. Having become stuck in closed loop of beloved ideas, they are, as it were, incapable of breaking the cycle. Here we see better than anywhere else the limitation of human nature, which cannot supersede itself even in the most brilliant and bright of its manifestations.

"Aimer, c'est comprendre," said Victor Hugo (to love is to understand). Love helps us take on the personality of our beloved. Having become one with our beloved, we can study him, so to speak, from within his own being.

"Listen, you heartless and cruel people," said St John Chrysostom, "you are not cruel to others, but to yourselves … When you nurture your malice, you are only preparing it for yourself, not for others."[29]

Is this not the state of the spirits of evil, who constantly wallow in enmity and hatred for everything good? Is this not the state of all people who do nothing but emulate the spirits of evil, feeding on the venom of their own poisoned heart? When this venom overwhelms our own soul, we clearly sense its demonic nature. Like a poisoned needle, it constantly pierces our soul, burning it with a fatal fire. We feel as though we will be consumed by this fire, but we continue to rip open old wounds, finding in this the pleasure of a perverted spiritual sensuality.

A certain woman of the world, in conversation with Metropolitan Philaret (Drozdov), asked him the following question, intending to provoke him: "Tell me, Vladyka, why did Christ appear first of all to a woman after His resurrection?" The Metropolitan, as was his custom, remained in thought for a while, then answered: "I suppose we must think that He wanted the news of His resurrection to spread faster." Of course, this is not the definitive answer to the question, but it certainly fit the character of the questioner, and the provoking lady unwillingly remained silent in confusion, having received the necessary lesson from the famous hierarch.

Whoever wants to be fair to other people should try to value people not by their negative qualities, but their positive ones. In other words, he should focus not on what they lack, but what they possess, even in the smallest degree.

Even the greatest minds usually speak with us as equals to equals, while the holy writers of the books of the Bible stand always at an unreachable height, being separated from us by a distance that man's natural reason will never be able to overcome.

Two feelings take hold of us at the cusp of every new year. On the one hand, we feel sorry for ourselves because another part of our earthly life has been ripped from us irrecoverably. On the other hand, we have a vivid sense of the continuity of time when we see that one year unnoticeably flows into the next. At such moments, we are involuntarily amazed at the mighty breath of eternity, of the endlessness of life.

"If a truth is initially persecuted, then it inevitably comes to be acknowledged even by the persecutors." Not a day goes by that this confession of the Great Sufferer for truth, St Athanasius the Great, is not once again proved to be true. The entire history of the Church is a constant triumph of truth persecuted. On every page of its history the immortal words of Zerubbabel are written down: "But the truth abides and is strong forever" (1 Ezra 4:38).

The eyes of a child begin to close at the repetitive melody of his nanny. In the same way, the monotonous rhythm of life gradually puts a person to sleep, and he falls asleep, striving for inner peace.

If we take into account that nearly a third of a person's life is spend in physical sleep, while the greater part of his waking hours are passed automatically, in habitual and almost mechanical motions, how much time does a person actually live on this earth in a fully conscious state?

Why is a state of doubt so torturous for us? Because it is not merely a disease, but the decomposition of the soul as it is ripped in pieces. Doubt kills our normal spiritual life, plunges us into darkness, and leads to despair. A person can bear the heaviest of sorrows, all possible deprivations and offenses, but not the torture of inner cleavage—that internecine warfare of our spirit battling itself. It is like a scorpion that stabs itself with its own venomous stinger. Exhausted by such a heavy trial, which not only ascetics, but even poets ascribed to the demons, the sufferer is ready to call down on himself an early death in order to find consolation in death's cold embrace. The question—to be or not to be—that Hamlet asked so poignantly most often arises in a soul ripped in half by the poison of doubt.

Some poems in Ivan Turgenev's works, written already with a hand weakening from old age, reveal a true confession of his heart. Like the withering trees of autumn, these poems are replete with melancholy and sorrow, those fellow travelers of the twilight years. Turgenev did not have Tolstoy's bravery and could not stare death in the face. Predominantly a champion and servant of the flesh, he wanted to hide from the threatening image of death in reveries of those fresh, sweet-smelling flowers that lined the path of his carefree and luxurious early life.

The main source of the power of our speech is contained first of all in the strength of our inner conviction. This can be proven with many examples. Simple people often cry when they hear a sermon that they don't even understand, solely because they are touched by the sincerity of the speaker's tone and the exalted nature of his spiritual emotion. When Peter the Hermit called everyone to the cause of freeing the Tomb of the Lord, he overwhelmed thousands of hearts with his speaking, although his language was completely foreign and incomprehensible to them. Evidently, our speech is capable of captivating people sometimes directly through the beauty of our emotions. In such cases, we are like instrumental music with no words.

Evil in its essence is so repulsive to us that it does not dare approach us in its actual form, with no mask. Thus, Satan often takes the form of "angel of light" (2 Corinthians 11:14). All temptations are in essence fakes, built on delusions created by our external or internal senses. Any temptation strives to replace truth with gilded delusion, true light with mirages. Temptation presents vice and passion, if not masquerading as virtues, then at the very least decorated with the halo of freedom and the tinge of sin's transitory pleasure.

All people live and nurture hope, something that the poet called the "god of coming days."[30] Often hope alone illumines the dark days of our life. The sick man hopes to become well, old age hopes to become younger and stronger, the pauper hopes to be freed from the oppressive vise of want. Every tired sojourner of this world says to himself: "Just wait a moment, you will rest as well."[31] How terrible it is for the person in whose heart the light of truth has become extinguished. Despair is just as terrible as spiritual death. Hell will be terrible because there will be no hope in it.

Our soul, distracted with constantly changing impressions during the course of the day, collects itself with the coming of night. This is why the night hours are considered the most opportune time for prayer, focused mental work, or any spiritual work in general. Unfortunately, the night is not only the domain of works of light, but it also provides a cover of darkness for works of evil that, like some predators and reptiles, are afraid to show themselves in the light of the sun.

It is much easier for a tall person to bend down to a short person than it is for a short person to reach up to a tall one. Generous people never forget this simple and noble rule of behavior with reference to the poor.

Kant was the first to make the observation that a person is capable not only of sorrow for his homeland, but he can also suffer from another disease—nostalgia for a foreign land. No matter where a person is, he is everywhere hemmed in, and something is always lacking.

"It is a common saying that a man needs only six feet of land," said Anton Chekhov through one of his protagonists. "But surely a corpse wants that, not a man … A man needs, not six feet of land, not a farm, but the whole earth, all Nature, where in full liberty he can display all the properties and qualities of the free spirit."[32]

But one can take this thought even further and say that a human soul is greater than the cosmos itself, and nowhere in it can the soul find a place of rest.

It is remarkable that a person can sorrow even in the midst of joys, that even in sorrows he dreams of days of consolation, but when these days do come, he does not want to rest in them, desiring still new, untasted pleasures. Never content with the present, he is able only to find worth in a happiness of dreams or remembrances of days long past.

> And like an orphan, like an orphan
> You wander on through fading days
> A man of pride and self-esteem,
> No place to rest along the way.[33]
> —Alexander Blok

While the best and often strictest judge of a work of literature is the author himself, he dares not rely on his judgment alone, and he anxiously awaits society's response. Apparently, even he finds a critique necessary, a common appreciation of his ideas to give them a stamp of truth.

"I sleep, but my heart keeps watch" (Song of Songs 5:2).

There is a certain kind of subtle sleep-state when the soul overcomes the inertness of the body and seems to separate temporarily from it, acquiring an especially clear vision. Metropolitan Philaret called this state "dream-vigilance."

Sin that rules in the world poisons the very source of our joy, mixing its well-known bitterness into its streams. Therefore joy often dies even before it is born, as Shakespeare said.

There was no barrier between man and God in Eden. The heart of man freely and joyfully turned to his Creator, as a flower turns to the sun. Every movement, every word, every thought of the first people was a song of praise directed at the Throne of the Most High. In the same way, the soul of a child, full of purity and innocence, is like holy music before God. In childhood, we need neither fasting nor asceticism in order to warm up religious emotions within ourselves. The prayer of a child pours just as freely and naturally as a request to his mother or father, as the sound of a skylark that bathes in the rays of the summer sun, as the sweet smell of a morning flower, ascending toward the heavens like incense.

A lack of self-contentment that pushes us forward toward perfection brings us much more benefit than dimwitted self-satisfaction, which is always a sign of spiritual stagnation. John Stuart Mill expressed this in somewhat crude, but essentially true, language: "It is better to be a human being dissatisfied than a pig satisfied."[34]

To those luminaries who are subjected to unfair attacks and slander from those who envy them or wish them ill, it would be useful to remember the consoling Japanese proverb: "Stones are hurled at a tree with much fruit."

Martin Luther, fighting against the monolithic authority of the Pope, did not have much respect for society either, calling it "Mister *omnes* [everyone], having no reason."

Talleyrand [Charles-Maurice de Talleyrand-Périgord] once said, "It was worse than a crime, it was a blunder."[35] Talleyrand was transformed by the Revolution from a bishop to a state diplomat. Here, of course, he reveals his well-known amoral mindset, which considered that the ends justified the means. However, if we keep in mind that here he has in mind people of high social position, whose mistakes are of historical import and can often be an irremediable sin before entire nations, or even the whole world, then perhaps this phrase does have a modicum of truth to it.

One cannot touch the tree of the knowledge of good and evil without being punished. The forbidden fruit always leaves a bitter aftertaste, which we cannot wash out often for the rest of our life. Our eyes truly are opened after this, but only to see our spiritual nakedness and to acknowledge our fallenness.

The word "parable" (parimio), literally translated from the Greek, means "located by the road." In ancient times, it was not uncommon for such pithy sayings to be written down and posted at intersections of roads for the edification of passers-by. It is a pity that this good custom is no longer kept in our time, along with much else that our patriarchal past has left us. Our modern-day shrieking commercialism uses the same path of psychic suggestion, but of course, for completely different purposes.

Many laugh when they are reminded of truisms, but these truisms have only become commonplace because they serve to remind us of eternal lessons for mankind, in whatever age.

"In this, indeed, does the remarkable quality of every true talent consist," said Tolstoy in his wonderful introduction to the works of Maupassant, "so long as it does not do violence to itself under the influence of a false theory, that it teaches its possessor, leads him on over the path of moral development, makes him love what is worth of love, and hate what is worthy of hatred ... The bearer of talent,—man,—may make mistakes, but the talent, as soon as the reins are given to it, as was done by Maupassant in his stories, will reveal and lay bare the subject and will make the writer love it, if it is worth of love, and hate it, if it is worthy of hatred."[36] The truth of these words would not be so obvious, had not Tolstoy proved their truth with his own example. The talent given him from Above was his most trusty guide to finding the true path, revealing to him genuine artistic and existential truth, but only when he "gave the reins" to it. Unfortunately, blinded by "the influence of false theories," Tolstoy often did violence to his own talent, and then his thought went off the right path and led him to a dead end, from which he could not find his way, no matter how hard he strained his uncommon mind.

That which comes forth unhindered from the pen of a writer, influenced by inner inspiration or a strong external stimulus, unwillingly captivates us with its power and liveliness. A thought that is passed through the crucible of rational thought, with its fresh aroma and warmth, becomes dry and distant. However, we must not always trust the first suggestion of our mind and heart. It is a wise rule to "measure seven times, and cut only once," instead of following the principle of Pontius Pilate: "What I have written, I have written" (John 19:22).

When I hear general praise for someone's mind without reference to his moral accomplishments, I involuntarily remember the words from Genesis: "Now the serpent was more cunning than all the wild animals the Lord God made on the earth" (Genesis 3:1).

No one can surpass the shrewdness of the Fallen Angel, whom some of the Holy Fathers wisely called "the seven thousand year old man." Despite this, hardly anyone would be foolish enough to envy him his laurels.

"I gave my heart to seek out and to prepare myself in wisdom concerning all the things done under heaven; for God has given painful distraction to the sons of men to be occupied therewith" (Ecclesiastes 1:13).

This is the lot of all who seeks wisdom. They go the way of intense spiritual asceticism (*podvig*). A great thought is borne in the soul, like a mother carrying a child in her womb, and is born often with the same kind of suffering, and the same kind of joy that no longer remembers pain after the new word has been spoken.

What is truth and what is rightness?[37] In Russian, the word truth (*istina*) comes from the word "*istoe*," meaning the agreement (similarity) of an object with itself, with its prototype or its original idea. Rightness (*pravda*) is related to the concept of moral order. It indicates our responsibility to fairly and honorably relate to the truth, and to follow it. One can know the truth and at the same time maintain it incorrectly (i.e., not submit to it). This is what the Apostle Paul accused the Roman pagans of doing. As for beauty, it is the effulgence of both truth and rightness.

To see how a person who has been marked by Providence falls from the high place assigned to him; to see how he suffers because of his greatness, his glory, his very self; to see how his inner source of living water withers, with which he fed and revived many; to see how the light of his creativity darkens and how his priestly calling becomes merely a profession—all these make a truly tragic spectacle, which Nikolai Gogol depicted with such creative power in his "Portrait":

> His life was already approaching the period when everything which suggests impulse contracts within a man; when a powerful chord appeals more feebly to the spirit; when the touch of beauty no longer converts virgin strength into fire and flame, but when all the burnt-out sentiments become more vulnerable to the sound of gold …[38]

Such a sad fate is not only the lot of the artist but of everyone who is called to be the salt of the earth and a light to the world if they stifle the spirit within themselves.

Whoever has seen children grow up knows that only during childhood does a person actually experience the reality of complete equality among all people. The heir to the throne plays with the son of his lowest servant, without demanding any preference, considering his friend to be his equal. In the schools we even see unforced equality and brotherhood among the students, even if they belong to entirely different social classes. Competition and fighting among people only begin when they start on the path of everyday life, in order to beat someone else to the finish line in the race toward earthly good things. Does this not mean that in the beginning of human history, in the time of its golden childhood, there was no social inequality, and that separation into a class system only began when people left this golden childhood and began to fight for survival? Sin is the primogenitor of all evil in the world, and sin was the first to create a rich man and a poor man, a master and a slave. To this day, sin remains the foundation for anything abnormal in the social order, anything that is oppressive and torturous for all. However, sin will not be uprooted until the end, not while its own primogenitor—that is, evil—still remains, having entered the world together with the fall of man.

A certain historian of rhetoric accurately writes that no matter what the talent of the orator, his speech, if it is not prepared and filled with the necessary content, will always be like a fountain with no water in it. Instead of a stream of words like water, he will utter nothing but the hissing sound of air traveling through pipes. False pathos is not only useless in hiding the paucity of a speech's actual content, but it will sooner bring even more attention to the inner weakness and emptiness of the speaker's thoughts.

Sorrow by its very nature is more profound than joy. It purifies our spiritual vision and helps our spiritual eyes gain insight into the mysteries of existence. On the contrary, happiness quickly makes a person arrogant and frivolous, capable only of skimming over the surface of things, without going into their deeper meaning. Therefore, the poet said: "I want to live: in order to think and suffer."[39]

While reading *Hamlet*, many perhaps are amazed by the scene depicting the gravedigger as he digs a grave, singing carelessly all the while. But this is merely a banal result of professional habit:

> Habit was given us in distress
> By Heaven in lieu of happiness.[40]

But habit is also capable of turning a human being into an apathetic automaton, killing in him any sensitivity, and sometimes killing his very soul.

A wasteful emptiness in life never goes unpunished in our inner spiritual world. Such wastefulness not only turns our spiritual world into an empty desert, but harms it directly, leaving it exposed to vain, carnal thoughts and all kinds of sins. One famous preacher said that if our soul was like a soundless instrument that remains silent when no one plays on it, then we could leave it alone without harm. But our soul is more like a field that, if left untilled, is soon covered with harmful weeds.

Some writers who please us in our youth cease to do so in later years. This means that we have outgrown them with age; however, some writers only become interesting to us as we slowly develop spiritually and become able to appreciate their profound thoughts and moods. While they were incomprehensible to us in our youth, they reveal themselves to our soul in their full power and meaning only with the light of the deeper understanding that comes with more mature years.

Diogenes, as is well known, would walk around in the middle of the day with a lantern, searching for an honest man. But here is what a more ancient and doubtless much wiser man[41] said of himself: "… Adding one thing to the other to find out the reason, which my soul still seeks, but cannot find: I found one man among a thousand, but a woman among all these, I have not found. Except behold, I found this, that God makes man upright, but they have sought out many schemes" (Ecclesiastes 7:27–29).

The hypnosis of another's thoughts sometimes so rules over us that it forces us occasionally to avoid close contact with people who have convictions far different from our own, if we want to maintain the purity and distinctiveness of our own worldview.

The words "human being" and "mortal" have long become synonymous. Death became one of the essential qualities of human nature and is for us something no less real than life itself. Life leads inexorably toward death by gradual withering, until the spirit leaves the body, which then falls apart completely. A certain English writer had this to say on the matter: "Mortality only is immortal and the law of change is the only constant law."

Even from the womb, a baby comes out with a sickly cry, as though bursting from a grave. But that same death, from which he flees as he bursts onto God's earth, already watches him at the threshold of earthly existence. This weak creature, in which the light of life barely burns, from his very first day must battle for survival. A thousand threats lie in his path.

Every person walks through life like a prisoner condemned to execution even before birth, every minute awaiting the carrying out of the sentence. However, we can never become comfortable with the thought of death, from which our entire being recoils. We all know that we must die, but we do not believe it. Nearly every day we watch our loved ones go to the next life, but we continue to think that this law does not concern us, and we will not follow in the footsteps of the entire earth. And when death comes face to face with us, we try to wave it away as though it were merely a terrifying phantom, until it lays its inexorable, cold hand on us. No one doubts that death is the worst calamity for all that lives. Implacable and merciless, it comes to a person at any age, it destroys the harmony of others' lives, it tears apart the most cherished and gentle attachments, it destroys our best-laid earthly plans and hopes, and it covers the momentary smile of life with the cold darkness of the grave. It enacted the law of decomposition, under which all of creation suffers, awaiting its renewal. But in this most horrible evil is hidden the greatest good for fallen man.

Death is necessary in the general economy of the cosmos after sin entered the world, exacting its horrifying tribute. Death is good for the world first of all because it cuts off evil, which strives—as does good—to strengthen itself and develop eternally. If the crimes of hardened villains were never ceased by the fateful blow of death's hand, they would every day become worse and worse, eventually becoming horrors not only to others but to themselves as well, becoming as cruel and hardened as demons. Life on earth would then become unbearable and would truly become hell. The lot of righteous and virtuous people would then become especially difficult, because they would be forced to suffer for an endlessly long time in a depraved society, as Lot lived among the Sodomites. Death gives them rest from their labors and temptations and forever confirms all the good that we have gathered during our life.

On the other hand, it takes away the heaviness of life from people who have been weakened by time and debilitated by disease, who would otherwise walk like horrifying ghosts over the earth, turning the entire world into a huge hospital and becoming a burden for the younger generations.

> O death, your judgment is good to the man in need and failing in strength in his extreme old age, distracted by everything, and stubborn and short on patience. (Wisdom of Sirach 41:2)

The law of death removes or at least warns all these abnormalities of normal life, reinstating to it its necessary balance. Death truly is not only a mystery, but a sacrament for us. In it, something holy is revealed if we look at it as a great sacrifice brought for our sins. It is the fire that cleanses the earth, which has been defiled by the crimes of mankind. According to His wisdom, the Creator, after the fall of the first people, bound everyone to the law of death, in order to give everyone life in more abundance: "Unless a grain of wheat falls into the ground and dies, it remains alone; but if it dies, it produces much grain" (John 12:24). From a perishable seed, an imperishable life will arise, even more full and blessed than it was before the fall.

We have just as little courage to speak the truth to ourselves as to other people. In both cases, we prefer lies, flattery, and hypocrisy. The latter two are born from the former and are only a subspecies of it. A person is capable of being a hypocrite before his own conscience just as well as he does it before his friends. Tolstoy said that flattery often is required in friendship, as a kind of lubricant for its wheels.

Friedrich Nietzsche forever killed Utopian Socialism with one of his thundering aphorisms: "Equality to the equal, inequality to the unequal."[42] In actual fact, this is nothing more than a rephrasing of 3 Ezra 7:25[43]—"emptiness to the empty, fullness for the full." On his part, Aristotle found that "there is no greater inequality, no greater unfairness, than the equal treatment of unequals."[44] The principle of universal equality also contradicts natural law, because there is no equality in nature, as well as the requirements of moral rightness and justice, both of which strive to give to each according to his gifts and just deserts. A certain simple person who was gifted with clear common sense, upon hearing of the desire of socialists to divide all earthly goods equally among all people, asked with bewilderment, "How can they hope to achieve this? Because first of all they would have to divide the mind." The thought of this man, who was not clouded with any preconceived notions or theories, easily understood that which many wise men could not. The source of all capital is, first and foremost, man's work, and the productivity of any man is based on his theoretical and practical abilities, that is, his mind, his initiative, and the persistence of his character. We must always consider the parable of the talents and remember the eternal law of life, according to which the one who has will receive more, while the one who does not have will lose even that which he owns (Matthew 25:29).

The Kievan Era of Russian history has the same reference to the Muscovy period as childhood is related to adulthood. Kiev is the half-conscious state of Russian nationality, often dipping into legend and the "supermen" of Russian folklore.[45] Muscovy is already an active and fully conscious period of governmental and social development. This period is the maturity of the Russian national genius.

"I know that all this is nothing but rags, but still I am proud," wrote St Theophan the Recluse, a famous ascetic and theologian, describing his spiritual state after receiving a high state honor. This is the best answer to those who insist that to know evil for what it is means to defeat it. No, the old man lives in us contrary to our own reason and will, and he is only defeated by the power of grace that makes us a new creation.

We would all like to bask in careless happiness, considering such a state nothing but good for ourselves, and we complain when days of worry or sorrow visit us. However, according to one Holy Father, "God in His wisdom sends us sorrows for our happiness." St John Chrysostom said, "In happiness, a man must consider himself a debtor before God, but in unhappiness—when he bears it without complaining, with reverence and prayer—God is his debtor."

A hardened human heart can be softened only with the fire of living faith, the warmth of love, the heat of inspiration, or the flame of angry denunciation, so long as that denunciation is not connected with a feeling of hatred and anger.

The tragedy of those who do not believe is that no person can fully convince himself that he is merely an animal. His own spiritual nature rebels against such a thought. It tells him that to reject God means "to impugn the dignity not of God, but of man himself,"[46] since man's dignity is founded only on the idea of the divine. Bending under the yoke of the merely apparent freedom of his rational mind, the religious skeptic unwillingly turns back to the sweet bonds of faith. "I am a tired rationalist," said Augustin Thierry, "I feel the need in a unerring authority; my tortured spirit needs rest." Another Augustine, from the early centuries of the Church, answers him, "Oh God, You created us for Yourself, and our soul and our unruly heart will not find rest, until it rests in You."[47]

In order not to fall into despair at the sight of the universal fading of religious inspiration, one must revive in oneself the faith in the constantly growing power of Christianity, in the victory of the Church over the world in the past, present, and future. One person said, "Faith in Christ is a force that cannot be defeated. Like the mercury in a thermometer, this force either rises or falls, but it never lessens." A similar thought was expressed by Aleksey Pleshcheyev, when he wrote the following poignant lines:

> O, children of a weak, distrustful age,
> Does not that Image, strong and great
> Remind you of the dignity of man
> And wake the slumbering will to action?
> Oh no, I won't believe it. Desire and vanity
> Have yet to quench in us the voice of truth.
> A day will come, Christ's might and sanity
> Will bring to new life to this decrepit world.[48]

In another poem, Pleshcheyev even begins to pray:

> Appear to us once more
> O Lord, descend to our poor world,
> Replete with sorrow and dismay.
> Proclaim aloud your Word Divine,
> Recall to life all those who went astray.

A long time ago, during the dawn of Christianity, Tertullian could boldly say to the pagans:

> We are but of yesterday, and we have filled every place among you—cities, islands, fortresses, towns, market-places, the very camp, tribes, companies, palace, senate, forum,—we have left nothing to you but the temples of your gods.[49]

Alas, in our days, after the passage of almost two thousand years after the triumph of Christianity, it is again being pushed out of the forums, senates, palaces, and other social and governmental institutions. Family is the last social force where the laws of Christ still hold strong. Contemporary governments are becoming increasingly secularized, returning to their pagan origins, while in international affairs, it is already considered naive and even comical to be guided by the morality of truth, righteousness, and love. The most important guiding force in international affairs is national pride and considerations of what may benefit the state, especially the latter. The golden calf has never before so openly ruled the world as today. If, as Shakespeare wrote, gold is always capable of turning "black white, foul fair, wrong right, base noble, old young, coward valiant,"[50] and if, according to Pushkin, it can "enslave" equally "willful genius and bloody crime,"[51] then nowadays it can truly rule over the minds and hearts of men unchallenged. It shakes and topples the thrones of the powerful, raising to power worthless people. It provoked external complications and wars and it ignited internecine conflicts, most terribly manifested in bloody revolution. There are no values that would not submit to it on the world market, where everything is bought and sold, first and foremost honor and conscience. Contemporary political and financial crises, caused first of all by man's fallen state, would seem to be the perfect warnings for mankind that it is rushing into the abyss. St Nikolai (Velimirovich) said, "God used a contemporary means to chastise contemporary men; He struck the banks, the exchanges, the finances, the currencies. He turned over the money-changers' tables all over the world, as He did once in the Temple at Jerusalem." However, mankind doesn't want to stop rushing forward on its fateful path and continues to celebrate a feast in the middle of the black plague.[52]

Strong ambition tends to sometimes dampen a person's self-love, but only because ambition is nothing more than a development and deepening of self-love. The lesser is here brought as a sacrifice to the greater.

Constant inner attentiveness is necessary to master one's own thoughts, feelings, emotional states. As soon as a person comes out of himself, so to speak, and begins to act "beside himself," he immediately loses control over himself.

When we walk with a head held high and don't want to bend our proud neck ourselves, the Lord, in His love for us, humbles us "with a mighty hand and an upstretched arm" (Psalm 135:12 (LXX)).

If you see before you a person with a face alight with pure joy, do not extinguish this light in him. Joy is a heavenly visitor; it is a feast of life that far too rarely visits us on this earth. Give freedom to these vivifying rays of the sun. They purify, illumine the souls of people, binding them to each other more tightly. Suppose that a sufferer rests from his pain for a brief moment, tomorrow the light will once again darken over his head, and he will once again awake to tears and sorrow. Days of sorrow drag on monotonously, while minutes of joy pass instantaneously, as though on wings. "No. This is too good to last long," we tell ourselves in such moments, not allowing ourselves to believe in our own happiness. Usually joy leaves us quickly because we become unworthy of it, for blessedness is the inheritance only of the pure and humble of soul and heart.

Many eminent rulers are required by their exalted position to learn the art of choosing worthy helpers. "Having placed each in his surest place, the ruler can glean from them a double harvest," said Frederick the Great. However, this does not diminish the importance of these great rulers for history. To have an ability to sense the worth in a person and single him out, indicating the best use for his talents, is itself a special talent of those in power. Furthermore, the real talent of a ruler lies in his ability to unite the disparate talents of his helpers under one idea and to direct them to a unified goal.

The psychology of the masses remains largely unexplored. Why do the most enlightened and moral people, when gathered together, often lose their personality and become an unruly mob, stooping to moral depths that they would never allow on their own? How is it possible that spiritual values counted together en masse are less than if counted individually? Why do people, like an ocean, remain immobile at the same time as their top layers are heaving in massive waves of revolution? Why do people, like an irrational flock, allow themselves to be led by their leaders, even when these are by far not the best of people, but rather merely the boldest and most impudent? Why is spiritual disease so easily spread from one to another in a mob, like rot in fruit piled on top of each other? Why is evil in human society generally more active than good? Why is the collective mind and conscience so insecure, so easily inclined to blindness, so easily blown to one side, then the other, by the rhetoric of demagogues? All these questions remain unanswered before mankind, despite all the efforts of psychologists and sociologists to answer them.

"It is unfair to punish small people as examples, because they are like trees that have no significant shadow," wrote Cardinal Richelieu in a letter to King Louis XIII, who was under the direct influence of the Cardinal for the entirety of his reign. This all-powerful government minister was not afraid of chopping down great oaks that left large shadows. He did not even spare the mother of the king, Maria de Medici, who, thanks to him, died a pauper in exile.

"God does not give the Spirit by measure" (John 3:34). When the Spirit touches our heart, then the limits of our nature expand, some kind of secret sources of knowledge are revealed, and before our eyes eternal horizons open up. Our thought and heart immediately seem to embrace the cosmos, and the human in us dissolves in the divine. Only in such moments can we feel the fullness and beauty of creation, only then do we truly live, and do not merely trudge along. But such flights of the Spirit are not safe for everyone. As with a balloonist who ascends too fast into the stratosphere, such a person's head can begin to spin, leaving him in danger of falling back down to earth. Saving us from ourselves, God does not leave us mortals too long at such spiritual heights. He takes away our wings, and we once again descend from the heavens to earth. Like a swollen river after a flood, our spiritual life once again returns to its usual ebb and flow. Yesterday's God-Man once again becomes a worm, and as before he beats the walls of his prison, striving once again for light and freedom. Even the saints experienced such occasional impoverishment and pain of the spirit, in order for them to better value grace's visitation.

A blabbing tongue is usually born of unbridled thought and unconstrained emotions. Therefore, it is just as likely to repulse us as a person who knows nothing of the discipline of propriety.

What attracts us in beauty is its form, that is, something ideal and spiritual at its heart, which finds a corresponding reflection in our own soul. Therefore, beauty preserves its allure only at a distance. As soon as we come close and try to touch it, the miraculous vision dissipates, and man sees before him nothing more than crude matter.

For as long as the earth has existed, there have been people of a "rightward" and "leftward" orientation. Between these two ways of viewing the world there is a metaphorical ridge, beyond which begins their war of principles. Both sides are inclined to go to extremes in this war, and not only the Left, but the Right also becomes dangerous when they, in the heat of battle, go beyond common sense.

Only in youth does life present a bright, smiling face. Afterward, its aspect becomes more focused, and only seldom is its strictness illumined with a smile.

A person who is used to sailing with the current moves forward without expending any energy, until his boat finally gets stuck on submerged rocks. Lulled to sleep by his lack of cares, he does not feel within himself any energy or strength of habit to go against the current, and so his boat inevitably crashes.

Some spiritual experiences are so profound that they truly seem to be beyond the natural order of things, being an echo of another, more exalted mode of perceiving the world that reveals itself to us in that moment.

Life is a great school that has continued for millennia. Every day enriches us with new lessons, according to the Scripture: "Day unto day uttereth speech, and night unto night showeth knowledge" (Psalm 18:3). The particularity of this practical knowledge is its foundation on experience, and science itself agrees that experiential evidence is the truest path to studying the truth.

Success and happiness always inspire a certain amount of superstitious fear in some people. They easily bow down before those whose star is rapidly on the rise. When these rising stars, having reached their zenith, begin to set, their admirer do not notice the fall, because they are still blinded by the afterglow, and the former chosen ones of fate can continue to reap the benefits for years to come. Their admirers do not want to see their fall only because they fear to break the enchantment that holds them.

"If we, people, only differ from animals in our ability to speak, then how highly should we honor those who supersede other people in the same way we supersede the animals!" A certain Roman orator had this to say about in praise of the word. Of course, he considered himself to have such an advantage over other people.

The essence of creativity becomes more understandable to us when abstract ideas are translated into concrete language. What is architecture? It is, according to Friedrich Schelling, "music in space, as it were a frozen music."[53] Another artistic authority said that "painting is silent poetry, while poetry is painting that speaks."[54]

Immanuel Kant said, "People whose lives are of the highest quality fear death the least."[55] History gives many examples proving this observation of the great philosopher.

Those experienced in the art of war sometimes say that whoever tries to outflank his enemy on the battlefield leaves his own flank exposed. This warning is worthy of remembrance not only in war. Its practical truth is constantly seen in everyday life, since life is a constant war, a constant series of flanking movements of certain people in relation to others. How often do we see that the Lord "catches the wise in their craftiness and subverts the counsel of the cunning" (Job 5:13).

We must not excessively abuse anything, even the striving for increased knowledge, in order to avoid "mental over-production," which wastes a person's spiritual energy. John Milton memorably said in *Paradise Lost*, Book VII:

> But Knowledge is as food, and needs no less
> Her Temperance over Appetite, to know
> In measure what the mind may well contain,
> Oppresses else with Surfet, and soon turns
> Wisdom to Folly, as Nourishment to Winde.

Any life experience never disappears without leaving a trace in our soul. This is one of the fortunate and at the same time unfortunate advantages of the human spirit. Thanks to this, we can relive bright and pleasant days long past in our memories. But we can also unwillingly remember long-ago experienced pain and grief. Sometimes we would rather we forget the past, but at other times we are ready to repeat Mikhail Lermontov's words:

> Now all is gone, but you remain with me
> Relief from pain, salvation in silence,
> My soul's repose, O holy memory.[56]

In life, one must always be ready to bear the cross of being a confessor of the faith, which requires an active and unflagging battle with evil and a courageous defense of the truth. To remain silent when a holy object is being desecrated means to be unfaithful to the faith and to become a participant in this crime. "You did not participate in the brazenness of the offenders?" asks St John Chrysostom. "For this I praise you, but you did not hinder their brazenness, and therefore you are worthy of condemnation. We will hear the same words from God if we will remain silent when others blaspheme and defame Him."

All foregone conclusions become hardened by force of habit, and since habit is the second nature of man, sometimes even the most enlightened and discerning of people are not lacking in this flaw that so often demeans them.

For true chastity, even a word is a kind of laying bare of the soul. Therefore, modesty prefers to keep silent, fearing that by the very sound of its own voice, as through a door opened from the inside, an ill-wishing eye might glimpse the inner sanctum of our heart. "Therefore, let your lips be like a closed flower-bud and let your word be longed for by others."[57]

Friendship, wherever it is found and in whatever form it manifests itself, is always founded on some kind of invisible affinity of souls. In the diversity of people surrounding us, our soul searches through an inner sense for a heart harmonious to itself, and it joins with him through gentle, mysterious bonds. Friendship, as love, knows no bounds of race or social position, and it can befriend a shepherd to a king's son, as it joined David and Jonathan. Friendship always carries a pure, platonic character and in this sense supersedes romantic love, which is not always able to remain on such a height of purity. At the same time, its essence is related to love and often intertwines with it. A true friend is often more treasured and reliable than even one's own relatives, with whom we are only joined by bonds of flesh and blood. When we want to underline a special affinity for a family member, we often say: "He is not merely a father or a brother to me, but a friend as well."

"A faithful friend is a strong shelter, and he who finds one finds a treasure" (Wisdom of Sirach 6:14). Friendship flowers especially during youth, when our soul is still expanding, finding sympathy and resonance everywhere. This feeling can be called holy, for it is inculcated into our heart by the hand of the Creator. Even Christ the Saviour, who loved the whole world, chose His own close friends in St John the Theologian, Lazarus, and his sisters. When the bonds of friendship are torn by parting of the death of one of the friends, we always feel pain. It is fair to say that in each of these lost friends, we lose, as it were, a part of ourselves. The God-Man Himself unwillingly paid His tribute to this feeling when He wept over the tomb of dead Lazarus, thereby sanctifying the reverent and gentle feeling of true human friendship.

An avaricious man becomes used to measuring everything against the value of money, even spiritual values. He has no other mode of thinking. If "property," as Pope Leo XIII wrote in his famous bull *Rerum Novarum*, "is a continuation of the person," then to an avaricious man, his personality is, as it were, an extension of his property, which leaves a heavy stamp of materialism on his soul.

To understand one's own mistake before it is too late, and to reject it, is a sign of an enlightened mind and noble heart. Stubborn insistence on one's own mistaken opinions, on the contrary, is typical of a limited mind or a degenerate character. When Otto von Bismarck was once reprimanded in the Reichstag for changing his mind about an issue, he answered with his usual directness: "Only a moron doesn't change his mind when there is good reason to do so." French wit has long ago come up with a proverb, whose meaning is that foolish people want to equate themselves with God, Who alone does not change His mind.

When the Lord saw the world as it was created by Him to be such as it should be, that is, according to His pre-eternal providence, he found this to be "very good," truly beautiful. Sin destroyed this miraculous harmony, and the primeval beauty of the former cosmos dimmed. Untruth and evil, the children of sin, can never be beautiful. They are not capable of inspiring anything in us other than disgust.

"There is nothing beautiful other than the truth," the French say. One must have a degenerated imagination and a perverted aesthetic sense to see any kind of beauty in the father of lies and the first source of evil, the devil, whom—in the guise of Lucifer or Mephistopheles— many poets and artists, the high priests of the beautiful, have tried countless times to poeticize.

Sometimes we are given an opportunity to sense the coming of an especially sunny, joyful day in our life with some kind of inner sense. On the other hand, thanks to the same, intangible, subconscious feeling, we sometimes hear the heavy sound of the coming steps of coming sorrow, which already from a distance covers us with a dark fog. That and the other sense we usually call prescience.

People's personalities differ sometimes to extreme opposites. Some strive for peace and calm, fearing the least bit of conflict or misunderstanding with those around them; others, on the contrary, thirst for battle, which is the environment best suited for their existence. If they have no real antagonist, they create him in their imagination, and in the desire to throw him down, they glean the pathos needed for their words and actions. Sometimes, because of the dearth of material able to keep their inner fire going, it begins to fade for a time; then they immediately lose the energy that had inspired them and lower their wings, like a sailboat stuck in a sea with no wind.

To admire a beautiful veneer without considering what lies underneath is childish; an adult will treasure the worth of every thing and every person based first of all on what they are made of on the inside.

"Dead flies will corrupt the preparation of seasoned olive oil, and a little wisdom is more valuable than the glory of great foolishness" (Ecclesiastes 10:1). A person can live a life of spotless virtue for decades, and the world will never stop to notice. But should he trip but once, everyone begins talking about his fall and will never forget it. People in the cruelty of their hearts are incapable of emulating the mercy of God. They continue to defame and judge their fallen brother even after he has repented in this or that sin and even after he has repaired the damaged caused by it, having received forgiveness from God himself.

Every person, according to Schopenhauer, was beautiful or brilliant at least once. This happens usually in youth and lasts only as long as youth retains its sweet aroma of purity and innocence.

When Jean-Jacques Rousseau and Tolstoy rose up against culture and civilization, ascribing to them exclusively the perversion of the natural simplicity and purity of human customs, they were incorrect only in one respect: they excessively idolized natural man and forgot about the degenerative effect of sin and evil, whose poison every person bears within him from birth. However, in other ways they were completely correct. That nearness to nature indubitably saves the human heart from many temptations that lie in waiting to trap anyone living in the refined world of high culture—so full of conventions, lies, and hypocrisy—was also noticed by a certain enlightened Greek, a contemporary of Michael Paleologos, and consequently a witness of the fall of Byzantium. This man wrote: "Unfortunate is the fate of all governments, for everything good comes from the country, and at first shines brilliantly in the capital city, but everything rots in the city, and only sins and calamities return back to the country."

"I, as a sculptor, as a master of all things golden, carefully mold, carve out, and decorate in whatever way I can that chalice in which I will bring to my own lips the poison."[58] Here is a true confession of a member of the Russian intelligentsia, a quintessential example of which was Turgenev himself.

Refined self-poisoning is the fate of our (Russian) intelligentsia. It need not feel the flowering and aroma of life, so pleasant to people with a whole spirit. In this way a spider is able to glean poison from the same flower that gives a bee nectar.

They say that ideas rule the world. However, these ideas can remain for a long time in the sphere of abstract thought, not taking concrete form. Only when they become incarnate in flesh and blood, that is, take fire in the emotions and wills of people, do they become the great movers of human life.

The more expensive and exquisite the work of a jeweler, the more trimmings of gold or other precious materials will he have left over. It is the same in an art studio: one can always find an excess of unused details and sketches, many of which are quite valuable themselves. We see the same tableau in the laboratory of the soul of great thinkers and writers. They gather a great excess of unfinished thoughts and aphorisms that don't quite fit into their finished work. These remnants that fall from a rich table are often in themselves enough to feed many people who seek spiritual food.

Although we are profound realists by nature, desiring to see everything with our eyes and feel with our hands, we people still put our complete trust only in an ideal world that always remains true to itself and never lies to us, while remaining also invisible to us. Gustave Le Bon, a man who dedicated most of his life to studying social phenomena, came to the following instructive conclusion: "The dream, the ideal, the legend—in a word, the unreal—it is that which shapes history."[59]

Victor Hugo was even more categorical in his expression of the same truth, when he said, "O, Ideal, you alone exist."[60]

If you want to probe deeper into the soul of this or that writer, you must read his works with special attention. In them, as in a mirror, his own spiritual likeness is reflected. They nearly always create their heroes according to their own image and likeness, often placing in fictional mouths the confession of their own hearts.

The bright thought of an artist is just as capable of inspiring a person as noble, exalted feeling. Even in such a great poet as Schiller, the pathos of thought often outweighs the pathos of emotion.

When a genius helplessly battles against the minutiae of everyday life that oppress him, he reminds one of a lion entangled in a net. A small mouse in such a situation turns out to be stronger than the king of beasts. Thus a person of a middling, practical mind is often more conformable to life than a genius who always seems somehow not of this world.

Sickness is an anomaly that brings disorder not only into our own personal life, but to the lives of those surrounding us as well. Because of this reality, a sick person often unwillingly feels himself guilty before all for his sickness.

Truth, like the shining beacon in a lighthouse, rotates before us, show-ing first one side, then the other. It never shows itself to us in its entirety.

Time is not only the best healer for spiritual suffering, but also the "great critic," as Vissarion Belinsky called it: "Its wings flap over all the works of man, leaving only a few grains in its wake, while dis-persing much chaff in the wind." Truly we see with our own eyes how time reevaluates all values, dethrones authorities that seemed indisputable, and raises to the heights people who were not acknowl-edged during their own lifetime. The conservatism of human nature usually slows this process down, for it is painful for us to leave behind our habitual idols, even if we have been convinced that they no longer have their former significance.

Whoever has a certain talent tends to be the first himself to admire and take pleasure in that talent. He reminds one of a jeweler who takes delight in the multi-faceted brilliance of the gem he holds in his own hands.

Every person carries within himself his own *memento mori* in some form or another, and this reminder of death is useful for all. It mod-erates a person's pride and serves as a source of true wisdom for him. Tolstoy admitted that the thought of death revived him morally, forcing him to think about the question of the meaning of life. Ivan Bunin, in his turn, obtained "faith in God, a palpable sense of Him together with an understanding of death."[61]

For a righteous man, the law does not apply simply because it has long ago become his second nature; having absorbed its spirit, a holy man can sometimes even stand above the external strictures of the law. But such an advantage cannot be the inheritance of those who only have begun to step along the way of spiritual struggle. The beginner needs all external forms and rules of the law to determine his life, just as discipline is needed for a child and youth to form their character, just as a trellis is needed for a young tree. A certain enlightened monk, filled with divine experience, spoke a truly wise word: "Let us honor with reverent contemplation the freedom of action of the ancient monks, which came of their great success. Let us honor their freedom by reverently refusing to emulate it, acknowledging our own insufficiency."[62]

If it is at all intrinsic to our nature to cry over the one who leaves the world before having had a chance to fully develop his talents or fulfill his earthly calling, then this feeling becomes especially profound when we see the early death of a genius. We are ready to say with Pushkin:

> Like a cherubim from heaven,
> He brought us several songs of heaven,
> And having roused within us, creatures of the dust,
> Desire without wings, he flew away thereafter.[63]

The sea is a mystical, eternal element that spreads out before our gaze in a bright azure and then suddenly rises with threatening waves. The sea—always heaving its mighty chest in constant ebbs and flows—is the best image of the unfaithful and inconstant life of man. At the same time, it is also a symbol of endless eternity. Is this not why it so attracts our soul to itself, so that we feel a kind of kinship with this force that so personifies man's fate on earth?

True generosity is measured by how much a person is capable of humbling himself not only before those greater or equal to him, but also before those who are beneath him.

Joy is not simply an external appurtenance or decoration to life, as we usually think. Rather, it is inseparable from our life in its very essence. That humans and all living creatures were created for joy—that life and enjoyment are synonymous—is obvious from the joyful sight of a capering child, the cheerful play of young animals, the inspired and exalted song of a nightingale, and the entire miraculous symphony of spring, the bright triumph of nature renewed. Wherever fullness and wholeness of life is lacking, there is no complete joy. When life is wasted or full of disorder, then joy flees as well, instead of which we feel unwilling sorrow and heaviness of spirit.

Myths and legends often embody the spirit of history much more profoundly than historical facts themselves. Anyone who wishes to understand the past needs to listen intently to their voice.

Talents are given to people so that they can shine out to the world. Therefore, talents hurry to reveal themselves as early as possible in a person, as if they fear to lose time that is given to each mortal in small measure, even a genius. And like a duckling, barely come out of the egg, already runs toward the water, so inborn gifts already reveal themselves in childhood. Usually, a talent in the arts is the earliest to manifest itself and blossom. Mozart, at only three years old, began to play on the piano. Liszt began performing publicly at age ten. Count Alexei Tolstoy attempted his first poems at sixteen, training himself in the composition of rhyme and meter. Lermontov, at fifteen, wrote and edited the first version of his *Demon*, and Victor Hugo was

awarded by the French Academy for one of his written works while
he was still in school.

It would be fair to say that not a single great idea passed through the
world without great sacrifice. Truth always walks the *Via Dolorosa*,
dressed in rags. Those "of whom the world was not worthy. They
wandered in deserts and mountains, in dens and caves of the earth"
(Hebrews 11:38).

"You can knock on a locked door with prayer, but you should only
walk through an open door with advice." These words of Metropolitan Philaret can serve as a good warning for those who don't usually
follow such a rule.

Desiring to explain or justify this or that occurrence, especially anything for which we feel responsible, we often say: "This is the inexorable march of history." In actual fact there is nothing inexorable or
predetermined in the ebb and flow of history. History is the cooper-
ation of two free wills—the will of God and the will of man, and the
latter can go either in agreement with, or in opposition to, the former.
The movement of history depends on this; God gives us the freedom
to act according our own discretion even when it will result in our
own death. However, He never ceases to direct the general flow of
human life, constantly guiding it to the best possible goal.

Poverty if often full of worries and even brazen, but do we not ourselves make it thus, forcing it to knock loudly into the shut-up doors
of our heart? We need to have special sensitivity to poverty that hides

itself from the eyes of men, poverty that "cannot dig," and is "ashamed to beg" (Luke 16:3).

Changing colors like a chameleon is not only seen in some animals —who are merely following the law of their nature—but also is a certain kind of person whose ability to adapt to any situation has also become a kind of organic habit. However, these people can only be successful among other chameleons. Others know their real worth and never forget that a chameleon can assume any color except white.

In youth, a person is usually completely extroverted. He feasts the bright feast of spring and "hurries to live and rushes to feel."[64] Many different impressions, unfurling before him every day, leave him no time to summarize them and make any corresponding conclusions concerning them. As old age approaches, our thoughts of their own accord gather themselves within us, and our cooled-off mind begins to make concrete conclusions about life's experiences.

At the same time, during these later years, we begin to simplify our interactions with the people surrounding us, and this is not only because in old age we have to economize our reserves of energy, but also because old age is already replete with life, and for it there is nothing new under the sun, and its gaze unwillingly begins to turn to another world.

No one ever assigned himself the great project of expressing Russian everyday philosophy through proverbs. Such a philosophy would be lacking in any idealization and would simply reflect how the soul of the people is in reality, that is, with all of the people's advantages and deficiencies. Perhaps we would find in such a collection of proverbs practical explanations of many situations from our own lives that leave us dumbfounded.

Whoever has not descended to the depths of humiliation, whoever has not been burned in the fires of suffering, whoever has not looked at the face of death does not know many mysteries of existence. This person has not even yet understood the true meaning of his own life.

By reading this prayer belonging to the first half of his life, which he wrote down in his personal journal, dated May 13, 1854, we can clearly see how much Tolstoy betrayed himself in the second half of his long life—when he created his own religion, his own gospel, in which, according to the witty observation of his friend B. Chicherin, he put himself in the place of Christ:

> My prayer: I believe in One, Almighty, and Good God, in retribution for our deeds, I desire to believe in the religion of my fathers and to respect it.
>
> "Our Father," etc. "For the rest and salvation of our parents."
>
> I thank you, Lord, for your mercy, for this, for that, for that … (in addition, remember everything that brought you joy).
>
> I ask that you send me good intentions and thoughts, and give me joy and success in them. Help me correct my failings. Deliver me from sicknesses, suffering, arguments, and humiliation. Grant me to live and to die in firm faith and hope in You, with love for others and from others, in usefulness to my neighbor. Grant that I may do good and avoid evil. But whether it be good or ill with me, may Your all-holy will be done. Give me true goodness.
>
> Lord have mercy, Lord have mercy, Lord have mercy.

In the Apostolic Constitutions, the following words are put into the mouth of the Apostle Paul: "Be ashamed, all you who keep for yourselves that which belongs to another. Emulate the grace of God given equally to all and then there will be no poor man left."

Pearls do not float on the surface of the sea. One has to dive to the bottom to find them. The same can be said of spiritual treasures. They are found only in the secret depths of our existence, from the depths of that mystery that is called the human soul.

Many capable people "throw themselves around," as the witty folk proverb has it. They are not capable of mastering their own energies and potential to concentrate it on a specific goal. It is useful to pin such characters down or put them in a vise, so to speak, so that they can come up with something productive or useful for society.

Not according to our own will are we given gifts of the Spirit freely, without any deserving on our part. However, we must strive to become worthy of the treasures that have been entrusted to us. It will be terrible for the one who bears a heavenly gift in an unclean vessel, using it to serve his own passions and vices, or simply playing with them frivolously, like a child playing with an expensive diamond. Wasting one's talent without bringing fruit is as reprehensible as leaving it unused. It is even more criminal to scoff at it, to pervert its use and nature. This is the same as pouring holy oil into the dirt and stomping on it with one's feet.

It is remarkable that the first worshipers of the newly born Saviour were shepherds, true children of nature, who could give Him no more than the treasures of their opened hearts, full of simplicity, faith, and humility. Much later did the magi come from the East, replete with learned wisdom, to lay at the feet of the God-Child gold, frankincense, myrrh, along with their reverent joy. They had to travel a long way before they could reach Judea, and even in Jerusalem they could not immediately find the birthplace of the King of the Jews. Does not this tell us that simplicity of heart and profound, well-intentioned erudition both alike lead to Christ? But the first path is more direct, shorter, and truer than the second. Shepherds are led by the Angels without any mediation, while the magi must learn from the speechless star and Herod with the scribes and elders of the Jews. They reached their goal only after difficulties and even dangers, and they did not hear the heavenly choir singing over the earth: "Glory to God in the Highest, and on earth peace to men of good will."

The illusion of sensual pleasures is apparent when we consider that they give fulfillment to a person only for a moment, and then they immediately inspire in him a burning sense of remorse, joined with repulsion to the object of one's passion. When Amnon, the son of David, in a fit of sexual passions dared to violate his own half-sister Tamar, immediately afterward he "hated her exceedingly, so much so that the intense hatred he bore against her was greater than the love with which he at first loved her" (2 Kingdoms 13:15). Thus violated nature took its own revenge and forced Amnon to feel the full bitterness that hides at the heart of any sinful desire.

An intimation of God's heavenly paradise is contained for the artist in art, and by that alone is it higher than all else. But by as much as triumphant rest is grander than every earthly emotion, by so much is the lofty creation of art higher than everything else on earth. Sacrifice everything to it, and love it with passion— not with the passion breathing with earthly desire, but a peaceful, heavenly passion. It cannot plant discord in the spirit, but ascends, like a resounding prayer, eternally to God.[65]

With these words of his artist-protagonist, Gogol muses on the true character of art. The brilliant prophet-writer already foresaw the coming storm of passions in the Russian soul, which would decide to put "deconstruction higher than creation" and force all forms of art—including the creative pen of the writer—to serve not calm and peace, but the roiling of discontent in the soul, as well as fratricide and hatred.

There have been many arguments about whether Christianity is essentially pessimistic or optimistic. Of course, it doesn't fit either category well, and stands above both.

Christianity mourns sin and evil that have lowered us from spiritual heights, but at the same time it triumphs over its ultimate victory over both. In other words, Christian sorrow imperceptibly becomes joy, and all the contradictions of life are resolved in a perfect harmony, a final chord accompanying the hymn of the saved:

> Alleluia! Salvation and glory and honor and power belong to the Lord our God! For true and righteous are His judgments.... Let us be glad and rejoice and give Him glory, for the marriage of the Lamb has come ... (Revelation 19:1–2, 7)

What a strange creature is man, who is ready to stake everything, even his own life, on chance, and even finds a kind of pleasure in this. This temptation is something that no other living creature on earth experiences. Man alone frivolously wants to throw his entire fate, like a coin, into the abyss, in order to try to catch it again before it lands. Worries associated with risk are the main attraction of such apparently mad, but infectious to many, experiences. Our poet long ago already noticed this strange characteristic of the human heart, and expressed it in his famous lines:

> Everything that threatens life
> Is, unaccountably, with pleasures rife
> For hearts condemned to death.[66]

Nothing gives the human word such power as the chastity of great and genuine feeling coming from the deepest part of the heart, restrained by a great sense of moderation.

The impression left by such a speech is directly proportional to that potential energy that it keeps within itself, which we value even more because this lava seething within is directed by man's will preventing it from exploding outward.

Having completed the turn of his life, a man once more returns to his starting point, that is, childhood.

We have long become accustomed to comparing old age with childhood. The similarity between them is not only expressed in the physical weakness and helplessness common to both, but also in the brightness and purity of soul evident both in old people and children, as well as in the directness of their entire spiritual life, their simplified interaction with those surrounding them, and, finally, in their excessive, irrepressible willingness to talk.

A tall man has no need to push himself forward: he is already visible to all. A short man, on the contrary, stands on tiptoes and screams loudest concerning himself, being afraid no one will notice him.

Children who try to appear older than they are act in the same way.

Therefore, it is easy to understand why lesser nations try with all their might to appear significant, and why in general nationalistic pride is often inversely proportional to the actual importance of a nation on the world stage.

Whoever wants to know how the Bible looks at human wisdom—and, consequently, culture in general, as long as it does not seek to become an end in itself and separate from religion—should read the following:

> The Lord gave discernment to Solomon, exceedingly great wisdom and a heart as broad as the sand beside the sea. Thus Solomon increased beyond the understanding of all the ancient men, even beyond all the learned men of Egypt ... Solomon spoke three thousand parables, and there were five thousand of his songs. He spoke about wood from the cedars in Lebanon, and the hyssop that grows out through the wall; and he spoke about cattle, birds, reptiles, and fish. So all the people came to hear Solomon's wisdom, and he received gifts from all the kings of the earth who heard his wisdom. (3 Kingdoms 5:5–10)
>
> How wise you were [Solomon] in your youth, and filled with understanding like a river. Your soul covered the earth, and you were filled with the parables of riddles. Your name was known to islands far away, and you were loved for your peace and for you songs, proverbs, and parables; nations marveled at you because of your interpretations. (Wisdom of Sirach 47:14–17)
>
> Love it [wisdom] and it will keep you. Secure it, and it shall exalt you; honor it, that it may embrace you, and give your head a crown of graces, and cover you with a crown of delight. (Proverbs 4:6–8)

Youth is always singing on the inside, and, like a harp, pours forth from itself quiet and bright melodies. It everywhere seeks for the sounds of heaven—revelations of complete harmony and ideal beauty, especially in man, the crown of creation. But youth's fate is cruel reality that crushes its dreams, bitterly disappoints them. Therefore, youth reminds us of a butterfly that flies straight at a flame in order to burn its wings.

It is strange that everything in nature strives for calm. Only its king—man—is constantly troubled and anxious, a state that only worsens with the development of civilization. He always "unquiet, seeks a storm, as though in stormy waters lies his calm."[67]

Throughout the ages, man always greedily devours the sources of knowledge available to him, but only to become convinced that he drinks from a broken vessel that not only does not quench his spiritual thirst, but rather makes it worse. The more the mind understands, the more man realizes that to encompass and fully comprehend all the mysteries of the world means the same thing as to scoop up an entire ocean with a ladle. This is the source of the lack of contentment and spiritual unrest that all people who seek knowledge feel even from the time of the Preacher: "Behold, I have become great, and have acquired wisdom beyond all before me in Jerusalem; and my heart has experienced much wisdom and knowledge. I gave my heart to know wisdom and knowledge, to learn proverbs and understanding. And this, too, was waywardness of spirit. For in the abundance of wisdom there is abundance of knowledge. And he who increases knowledge will increase suffering" (Ecclesiastes 1:16–18). "I only know that I know nothing," admitted Socrates, summarizing his wisdom, which to this day amazes the world.

In our own time, Goethe echoes him through the words of Faust. The knowledge of the pointlessness of his scientific and philosophical studies, to which he had dedicated his entire life, brought him to despair, and he was even ready to end his sufferings by his own hand, if he did not hear at the very last moment the choir of angels who praised the resurrection of Christ.

Carlyle, that brilliant and profound man, remained in reverent awe before the incomprehensible greatness of knowledge that humbles the pride of our reason:

> Science has done much for us; but it is a poor science that would hide from us the great deep sacred infinitude of Nescience [knowledge], whither we can never penetrate, on which all science swims as a mere superficial film. This world, after all our

science and sciences, is still a miracle; wonderful, inscrutable, *magical* and more, to whosoever will *think* of it.[68]

Finally, the author of *Decline of the West* (Oswald Spengler), the Ecclesiastes of our own times, through whose mouth moribund modern culture utters a death sentence over itself, said a truly wise and completely not skeptical word, when he said, "One must know much before one can become so wise that one begins to doubt the significance and worth of knowledge."[69]

When man imagines himself to be something, he quickly becomes nothing. When he considers himself to be nothing, he is capable of becoming everything.

It has long been noted that the pendulum of history careens from one extreme to another. Therefore, Luther was right when he said that mankind is like a drunk man on a horse: when you hold him up on one side, he falls down on the other.

An aphorism has this advantage: it underlines one essential thought and, having given it a finished formula, places it into the focal point of our consciousness. In this form, it is more easily digested, more fully absorbed, and more deeply impressed on our memory, than if it was one thought among many. Thus an oak that stands alone on a plain is much more impressive in its surroundings—and more vivid in our imagination—than a single oak in a forest of trees.

The ancients considered the aphorism to be the most appropriate form to express wisdom. We should remember the Book of Proverbs or the Wisdom of Solomon, which are series of separate aphorisms that are not otherwise connected with each other in any logical way.

"Tact is the mind of the heart." To such a pithy determination, worthy of the pen of Vasily Rozanov (in "Fallen Leaves"), one can only add a single word, to make it: "Tact is the mind of the noble heart."

There is the boldness of the searching mind, which was present even in the saints. This mind humbly knocks at the doors of the mystical until they open before him, allowing him communion with the very first sources of true wisdom. Then there is the brazenness of the proud, self-assertive human mind that seeks to destroy the barrier between us and the unknown world at any cost, until they themselves are crushed against the closed doors.

Any attempt by mortals to steal fire from heaven is always punished.

Like Prometheus, they are chained for their guilt to a cliff, losing their previous freedom of spiritual flight, or, like Nietzsche, are cast down into the abyss of madness. Then the words of the Scripture are fulfilled: "Has not God made foolish the wisdom of this world?" (1 Corinthians 1:20).

Our soul is a mirror in which the miraculous beauty of the creation is constantly reflected.

A certain French writer said, "The lily that you admire blossoms in your own heart and the roses that you look at decorate your own soul. All nature tells us of the greatness of the Heavenly Artist."

No less vividly does our own heart tell us of Him, as Victor Hugo poetically expressed in the following words: "When I listen to the voice of my heart, I hear a conversation between two people; in my soul there are two: He and I."

In prayer, as in spiritual life in general, a person can rise to different heights. St Nilus of Sinai defined true prayer in the following way: "When standing at prayer, if you will be above all other joys, then truly you have obtained prayer."

The great Shakespeare noticed a long time ago that one and the same thing costs either more or less depending on the person who owns it.

For a wise man who delves deeply into the hidden meaning of historical events or even just the passage of our everyday life, there is no blind chance in the world. According to the words of Metropolitan Philaret: "Only the blind viewers of the world ascribe to its passage their own blindness."

That which is customarily called chance is actually "a great force hidden in visible action, the shadow of the hand of the Omnipotent one, the incarnation of Providence."

Those who stand in the heights need to do very little to give happiness to others. Merely a smile, like a ray of the sun, is capable of reviving those to whom it is given.

St Jerome said, "When Origen spoke, all others seemed dumb."

Certain minds and talents are so tremendous that they oppress us with their greatness.

We stand in awe before them, as at the foot of a great mountain whose summit we will never see. It seems to us that the summit reaches to infinity.

"We have learned to defeat others with the conviction of our reason, but we have also learned how to accept lawful defeat," said one of the great teachers of the early Church. How many people are capable of such great-heartedness? Usually angry debates rarely result in the victory of truth, for "opinions," according to Dumas, "are like nails. The more you beat them, the deeper they are driven in." St Paul told Timothy to "avoid foolish and ignorant disputes, knowing that they generate strife" (2 Timothy 2:23).

The human soul may be likened to an ocean. We are capable of studying and measuring it only at its shores or peripheries, that is, its psycho-physical life. But the deeper we delve into its sacred depths, the harder it is to approach it with any kind of measure or quantity.

The creative life is not limited by any formulas or boundaries and cannot be weighed on the scales of exact science. Here the researcher must unwillingly put a seal on his mouth and take his shoes off his feet, for the limited here comes into contact with the Absolute. Vainly do we seek to plumb the depths of the human soul and see how a great thought is here born and nurtured. This is a mystery, sealed off with seven seals, that is just as inscrutable to us as to the author of the great thought. He is a riddle even to himself. As a landowner, he rises at night and looks, but does not know how the great seed grows within him, planted by the divine hand of the Creator.

The sharp edge of every difficult test sent to us from above consists in our lack of desire to first of all accept it with humility. Instead, we battle God within ourselves, desiring, as it were, to throw off the yoke He Himself laid down on us, like stubborn oxen. But as soon as we accept the will of Providence, our soul calms down and easily bears the burden of Christ.

Any cross, as Christian wisdom tells us, occurs in the intersection of our will with the divine will. Make the horizontal line parallel with the vertical, that is, direct your own will along the plane of the divine will, and there will no longer be a cross.

Profound sorrow is like physical suffering: it chains our thought completely to the source of our pain, thereby disordering the harmony of our spiritual life, narrowing our mental horizon, dulling our emotions, and even sometimes evoking a temporary paralysis of all our spiritual powers. It is not by accident that sometimes sorrow is compared to death. Like the lid of a coffin, it presses down on our soul, while joy expands it, as David constantly exclaims in his Psalms.

No glory is given for free; after it always comes something positive in the person. "Like a fiery tongue, it descends on the heads of the chosen."[70]

If it later leaves the ones it has chosen, it does so not because of caprice, but because the chosen one has begun to enjoy it too much, considering it an end in itself. Glory only relentlessly follows, like a shadow, those who despise it, working for the glory of God and for the good of mankind.

What is *byt* [to be/way of life]?[71] As the word itself shows, it is not an accidental phenomenon. Rather, it is what happens constantly; it is what constitutes our usual everyday life. In the same way that deposits of organic matter eventually decompose to become fertile soil, the deposits and crystallization of certain habits, customs, and views in life constitute its *byt* [being], which is a kind of spiritual soil that forms—if not completely, then at least for the most part—these or that unique characteristics of a given society and each of its members. The environment of our *byt* nourishes us from our cradle with its lifeblood, and through it enters into our spiritual organism. It can have an influence over an entire people, helping to determine a unique national character and giving a well-known stability to all of national life.

We accept the unique features of our *byt* subconsciously, like the air we breathe. Depending on whether these characteristics have more good or bad in them, they can aid either the improvement or the degeneration of our spiritual level. However, destroying the foundations of *byt* always causes a spiritual crisis, that is, an upheaval of the moral foundations of a society.

Although some rivers source from snowy mountain summits hidden in the clouds, they forget about their fountainheads as they descend into the plains. In the same way, our soul, which draws its best content from mankind's spiritual heights—so high, they even touch Heaven—later easily forgets about this and is ready to ascribe to itself that good which it took from others.

Together with Christ, such a brilliant light of reason arose in the world that today's schoolboy is truly wiser in many things than Socrates and Plato, and the least in the Kingdom of God is raised higher than the greatest minds of pre-Christian antiquity.

What can explain the antimony of our discursive reasoning? Pavel Florensky ascribes it to the insufficiency of the apparatus by which we complete this work (that is, our mind). Darkened by sin, our reasoning mind is like a mirror broken into many shards, which cannot give an exact reflection of an object. Only experiential, intuitive knowledge—especially that gained by contemplation in faith—resolves all these contradictions and reveals the world to us in all its wholeness and genuineness.

If Lermontov had written nothing other than his profound philosophical poem "Angel," he would already have been worthy of immortality. Here he depicts the eternal sorrow for our lost paradise, a sorrow that never leaves the human heart.

"It is boring on this earth, gentlemen," said Gogol, of course, not only in his own name. A dethroned king, exiled from his ancestral lands, man can never forget that which he ruled before, and so he always walks with a head bowed in grief.

Only during innocent childhood do the gates of Eden crack open before his gaze sometimes, but, having touched the forbidden fruit, he falls and once again is exiled from the garden of delights.

Chekhov described this childlike innocence, from which we distance ourselves through our personal, conscious sins, with the strokes of his pen.

"O, my childhood, O my purity!" exclaims one of the heroines of *The Cherry Orchard*. "I slept in this room, looked at the orchard through this window, awoke together with happiness every morning. And the orchard was exactly the same then as it is now! Nothing has changed. It is white, all white. O, my orchard, again you are young, full of happiness, the angels of heaven have not abandoned you. If you would only lift this heavy stone from my chest and shoulders! If only I could forget all that has passed!"

Every person has personal remembrances of this blossoming orchard, where the angels descended to speak to him. Every person remembers the joy that woke up with him every morning. And every person has a heavy stone on his soul that he would like to cast off to return to his previous freedom.

There is only one path to find this lost treasure again. The same great Lermontov indicates it for us:

Not having resurrected your soul's innocence,
You never will regain the Eden that you lost.[72]

Pascal was the first to call man "a thinking reed," showing at once his strength and his weakness. It seems to me that this definition is most appropriate for the Russian intelligentsia, which has long ago been inclined to consider itself the salt of the earth and the light of the world for its subtlety of thought, always a source of pride before other, less educated social classes. But having ripped their roots from the soil of organic folk culture, they quickly become reeds shaken by the wind. The weakness exhibited by our intelligentsia in the times of our greatest calamities is evident for all to see. This was payback for their overestimation of the importance of the intellect (which is where they received their nickname) at the cost of emotion and will, without which no creative impulse is possible in life.

Human genius is multifaceted to infinity. It shines with an infinite number of various rays of light. On this earth there are no two people that are as similar to one another as two drops of water. In each person we find something original. The intersection of the universally human and individually unique gives a stamp of extraordinary beauty to every thinking creature on this earth.

Youth is often a time of exuberant flowering, but it does not always keep its promises. As with trees in spring, some buds never germinate, remaining empty. You can only begin to estimate the number of fruits at a more mature age. Toward old age, a person definitively crystallizes. The authority of old age is partially based on this stability: it is a symbol of eternity.

Language is a direct impression of the soul of a people, while being at the same time its living history. The ancient Slavonic lexicon expressed this thought vividly when it made the words "tongue" and "nation" synonymous. A language, like any living organism, waxes and wanes. Its constituent parts are always interchanging; some of them become old and die, others—new and fresh—take their place and organically merge with the previously collected reserve of words and understandings. Every change in national psychology, every impression of this or that event in the historical life of a country inevitably leave their trace in the turning wheel of national language. Our great, free, and beautiful Russian language could only be created by a great nation with a profound soul, a glorious and majestic past. The musicality, flexibility, and beauty of our national language come not only from the fact that our people have lived close to nature—so full of various sounds like the breath of wind, the wail of storms, the whisper of forests, the songs of birds, the roars of animals—but first of all are an echo of inner harmony, so remarkable in the Russian soul. From the time that Bolshevism demeaned, dirtied, and cleaved the national soul, depriving it of its previous simplicity, wholeness, and splendor, our Russian language has become dirty and crude, having lost its intrinsic exaltedness, fluidity, and artistry of expression. The language empties and pales as much as the people who speak it slide into spiritual poverty. It becomes crudely flat or even becomes gibberish if a person descends to the level of the beasts.

In physical and spiritual nature, we often encounter a certain analogy. A first principle, like protoplasm, usually has a very small nucleus from which later grow entire multi-branched philosophical and scientific systems.

If we take into consideration that the word "culture" is etymologically derived from the religious "cultus," and if we remember that the first cities—prototypes of future governments such as the polis in ancient Greece and the *civitias* in Italy—were first of all religious communities, then we can easily conclude than not only culture, but civilization itself is born, sanctified, and fostered by religion. Johann Lavater seems to confirm this with his profound aphorism: "Religion is nothing else but genius."

"Do not boast about your inglorious glory, for you wanted to gain the fame of an orator, rather than a Christian." St Gregory the Theologian wrote this to St Gregory of Nyssa, chiding him for leaving his post of reader in the Church to take up a position of teacher of rhetoric after the end of Julian's persecutions. However, the latter soon returned his talent to the service of the Church, which crowned him for his profound writings with the nickname "Mind" (*nous*).

Socrates, Plato, and Aristotle—this noble generation of the greatest minds in human history—were all deeply religious, and the first two can be plainly called devout. Some Christian writers called them "Christians before Christ," and the early Church sometimes even included their images in the narthexes of early churches. Their entire worldview is based firmly on a religious foundation. Prayer was a constant fellow traveler through their lives, and it was the fruit-bearing source of the philosophical work of their minds. Socrates died with a prayer on his lips, and Plato is himself called "divine" for the exaltedness of his idealistic teaching to daily thank Heaven for allowing him to live during the time of Socrates.

A person has no more precious or irreparable capital than time, and one would have to be truly mad to waste it unproductively. "To kill time" is equally a sin before God, who gave us this talent for its best use, and a crime against ourselves, for days that are lost flow into the ocean of eternity and never return to us again. Then again, it is not time that flows past us, as we have become accustomed to think, but rather it is our own life that flows and passes by against the immovable backdrop of time. As props on a stage set, so in the historical arena, generations of men and entire nations pass by in a never-ending procession. The shorter the time of our earthly existence, the more must we try to redeem every moment of the time allotted to us, emulating in this respect the ascetics of old, tireless workers, who constantly went from prayer to spiritual reading, from spiritual reading to handiwork or other physical work, hardly ever giving their eyes a chance to rest. Other people of high spiritual level also treasured time, spending all their days and even their nights in tireless labors. Their rest was only in the change of the manner of work. Thus, Marcus Aurelius wrote his famous *Meditations* often in the field of battle, in his war tent. A certain famous government official, having hardly a single free moment, wrote to his friends only during the "leftovers" of his time, as he expressed it. "I have no time to live. The rejection of life's joys is a heavy tax that I pay to the future," said Balzac, who once spent thirty consecutive nights without sleep, hurrying to finish one of his works.

"A vain man," said Blessed Augustine, "constantly wastes precious time and struggles against Providence. He constantly wages inner warfare and his heart is tossed about by the winds of various passions. Attached to this life, he still wastes time, which seems to be burdening him; but then suddenly he begins to regret the time that has passed by …

He avoids boredom, but boredom, as though chained to his ankles, persecutes him unflaggingly for the whole of his life. In this way the Lord, as the All-wise Father, gives inner joy to those who know how to use time wisely and sends boredom as a punishment to those who do not treasure time and scatter it about uselessly … "

How many Christians—so often apathetic to their own faith—know that even Mohammad respected Christianity and admonished Christians to follow the Gospels without turning aside, since it is the foundation of their earthly prosperity and the source of their eternal blessedness.

"And if only the People of the Book had believed and feared Allah, We would have removed from them their misdeeds and admitted them to Gardens of Pleasure. And if only they upheld [the law of] the Torah, the Gospel, and what has been revealed to them from their Lord, they would have consumed [provision] from above them and from beneath their feet" (Koran 5:65–66).

"O People of the Scripture, you are [standing] on nothing until you uphold [the law of] the Torah, the Gospel, and what has been revealed to you from your Lord" (Koran 5:68).

One does not have to be a theologian to become convinced—merely flipping through the Koran, one finds many instances that the ancient Patriarchs and prophets are named, as well as Jesus, son of Mary, called to confirm the previous revelation and law—that Islam is merely "darkened Christianity."

Is not Islam's continued vitality in the East explained by those sparks of Evangelical light that still sparkle in the darkness of the Moslem faith? Islam is the only faith to have been born with a sword in hand, but its strength is not of course in the physical sword, but in its teaching—taken from the Bible—concerning God as Creator and Provider of the world, its teachings concerning the immortality of the soul and the righteous retribution after death. These teachings feed the hearts of millions of people, even in that remote and perverted refraction of the truth we find in the Koran.

One of the greatest contemplative minds of Christianity, St Gregory the Theologian, was at the same time a religious poet. His poems are imbued with lyricism. "Exhausted by disease," he writes, "I found joy in my poetry, like an old swan who recalls to himself the sound of his wings."

At the same time he wished his poetry to give young people and all who more than everything else love "the art of the word, as it were, a pleasant medicine, something attractive that also exhorts to the good."

✦ ✦ ✦

The foundation of religious feeling resides in humility before the Most High Being. This is not a passive or negative feeling, a kind of spiritual self-annihilation as some think.

On the contrary, humility is the creative principle of life. Seeming to destroy himself before God in the acknowledgment of his own unworthiness, a believer finds in Him the highest development and confirmation of his own personality. The Most High never remains a debtor to a person. When the latter lays on His altar the very freedom of his reason, as the highest of sacrifices he can offer his Creator and the God of minds, then the Lord immediately returns him this highest, God-like gift, but purified, enlightened, deepened, and truly free.

Look at the height of spiritual and intellectual flight that to the spirit-bearing Fathers and teachers of the Church, who have acquired true freedom in Christ.

"He who is spiritual judges all things" (1 Corinthians 2:15), while a natural genius often feels his own, to be direct, limitlessness. Biographers of Goethe say that he wanted to write an unusual epic poem called "Achilles" in order to outmatch Homer. However, he found himself powerless to fulfill this proud intention. It is also well known how weak and even pathetic Tolstoy was in his philosophical systems and even in the questions on purely practical everyday life.

Singing and music in general have a much deeper meaning and significance than is generally accepted. This is truly the language of nature that all living things speak—man, beasts, birds, even reptiles. A child expresses his desires with the music of his voice even before he knows how to express himself with words. Human speech, even in the highest stages of its development, has to avail itself of the music of the human voice in various intonations that give a beautiful curvature to mere flat words. How many depths of the spiritual life remain tortuously unutterable for the word! How often piercing sorrow overflows in cries and moans, while joy erupts in exclamations or song, only because both states are difficult to express in words. Sometimes we say of an angry man that he roars like a lion. Who does not know how musical dissonance tears at our hearing, as though cutting our very heart.

On the other hand, inspired music is capable of raising and moving our spirit much more than even the most eloquent speech. It not only feeds our emotions, but it stimulates the mind. Everyone knows what deep philosophy is inherent in the music of Wagner. Does this not mean that music—and especially singing—"is speech without articulate sounds, coming from some profound depth, which carries us to the very edge of infinity and holds us here for a few moments so that we can look at it."

In music there is always some kind of mystical power capable of tuning our soul to that or another mode, depending on its content. The following two examples from the Scriptures can illustrate this thought.

"So whenever the evil spirit was upon Saul, David would take a harp and play it with his hand. Then Saul would become well refreshed, and the evil spirit would depart from him" (1 Kingdoms 16:23). King Jehoram of Israel, King Jehoshaphat of Judah, and the king of Edom, having begun a campaign against Moab, asked Prophet Elisha to reveal the will of God concerning the result of the war. "But now bring me a harpist," said the prophet, and "when the harpist played, the hand of the Lord came upon him" (4 Kingdoms 3:15).

Prayer is the highest expression of the human spirit on earth, and it often strives to incarnate itself in harmonious music that serves not only as spectacular clothing, but also like wings that raise it to the heavens, where no one will silence its joyful song—the constant language of angels.

If such harmony did truly reign on earth, as it does in the heavens, then here also we would unceasingly sing the praises of the Creator of worlds, and human speech itself would remind us of music. We sometimes hear this kind of music in the speech of the common people, children, and pure youths, as well as all people with joy and peace in their hearts.

When the Holy Great Prince Vladimir, Equal to the Apostles, is likened to a merchant searching for a pearl of great price, this comparison has an especially deep meaning. As a wise collector, he searched long for this precious stone with no impurities, trying out various faiths, until he found it in Eastern Orthodoxy. He determined the worth of this pearl by its external beauty. In this, he and his emissaries saw the superiority of the Orthodox faith, and it was, of course, not merely an appreciation of aesthetic beauty (for which Byzantium was famous, having integrated the best artistic impulses of both East and West) but first of all an acknowledgment of its spiritual beauty that shone from within the external forms of Constantinople's majestic ecclesiastical art. In the Orthodox church, sacred chant and icon painting and architecture have a certain special rhythm that serves as a reflection of the heavens' eternal harmony. The masters of liturgical art had to become proficient not only in their work, but in the proper spirit of liturgy, to rise to the heights, to hear there the music of heaven, and to bring it back to earth. This heavenly music, engraved in all our ecclesiastical splendor, is much more accessible than the language of abstract theological concepts, and through this music first of all the Orthodox Church continues to fulfill its mission in the world.

Poverty and riches can both serve as the source of temptation for a person. If riches lead to arrogance and self-contentment, poverty—which Plato called the beginning of slavery—while it is not in itself a vice, can break and shake the firmness of a person's spirit, after which it is easy for him to fall to vice and sin.

Knowing this, the Old Testament wise man asked of the Lord only his daily bread, which the Lord himself commanded us to pray for in the Lord's prayer. "But give me neither riches nor poverty, and appoint what is necessary and sufficient for me; Lest being full, I become a liar and say, 'Who sees me?' Or being poor, I steal, and swear by the name of God" (Proverbs 30:8–9).

We have all become used to idealizing the ancient times, thinking that great men and heroic deeds occurred more often than now. Spencer believes that "this opinion is a result of historical perspective. In rows of columns standing at equal distance from each other, the columns farthest from us seem to stand closer to each other than the columns standing nearer to us. In the same way, the great events of the past seem to us to occur with greater frequency than in the present."

However, any person must agree with the fact that the spread of democratic and especially socialist ideas has made the soil of society less fruitful for a culture capable of producing great men. Like exotic plants, they need laborious care and a satisfactory spiritual atmosphere. Genius by its very nature is individualistic. Pushkin says this of genius: "Thou art a king; live thou alone. Walk the unfettered path, compelled by your free mind."[73] Wherever such a mind is forced into a Procrustean bed of preconceived theories, or whenever a genius is passed off democratically as one of the masses, genius unfailingly fades away.

"The beautiful must be majestic,"[74] but the majestic must be beautiful also, that is, first of all pure and bright. A criminal and amoral person cannot be called a hero, even if he did incredible deeds. Discoursing on Napoleon's morality, Tolstoy fairly upbraided those historians for whom "greatness seems to erase the distinction between good and evil. For us, with our Christ-given discernment, there can be nothing beyond this distinction. And there is no greatness where there is no simplicity, good, and truth."[75]

The ideal of Christianity is so high, illuminated, and all-encompassing that no unprejudiced mind or noble heart can help but bow down before it. "But where to do we see its true manifestation in real life?" ask those weak in faith or those with evil intentions. "Is this not the fate of every ideal?" one can answer them. It, as the sun, shines over our heads, enlightening our life's path, and humanity only gradually approaches it, rising up one step at a time. "The Kingdom of God and its truth," witnesses one theologian, "are still a historical reality only in the person of Christ Jesus. In us, the Kingdom becomes established not merely by the confession of ideal doctrines, but through experiential transfiguration of growth in grace . The more we graft ourselves to Christ, like a branch to the vine, the more we grow spiritually, until the day comes when a new heaven and a new earth will be revealed, and God will be all in all. This will be the time of the complete actualization of the Kingdom of Christ, promised to us in the Gospel."

"The most divine attribute of man is that he can do good," writes St Gregory the Theologian. "You can become God-like if you never miss an opportunity to do good to others."

"The measure of human law," said Thomas Aquinas, "must be its correspondence with justice, through which it becomes obvious that justice comes from the eternal law. When it deviates from justice, the law loses its power. It even ceased to be law, and become rather a kind of violence."

Everyone who is fated to live during a time of historical cataclysm is duty-bound to give an account of what he saw to the generations that follow him. This realization has led to the profusion of memoirs during our time. It is true that contemporaries cannot give a correct, pragmatic history of their time, because their experience of it was too subjective and lacked the needed perspective. However, no historian can recreate a tableau of a time that has passed if he has no written recollections of living witnesses of historical events. Through these human documents he comes into direct contact with a given era, he breathes its air, he is imbued with its spirit and through this he can communicate its living pulse, not a mere skeleton of historical facts.

Gogol searched long for truth on this earth, and, not having found it here, he directed his gaze to heaven. As a true Christian, he crucified himself to this world; he rejected worldly glory and even a part of his own talent. In this period of his life, when he rose to such a moral height, he was himself rejected by the world, that is, high society, which had lost its common language with him. As happens to all prophets, he remained alone among people, but his great prophecies were not forgotten by the Russian people or any of his literary descendants. He gave birth to an entire generation of Russian writers and poets, having determined his purpose as a writer to be not merely the depiction of life realistically, "as it was," so to speak, flattering the base tastes of depraved society, but rather to raise it to the heights and to serve the moral renewal of mankind. From him comes, like a golden string, the moral and religious tradition of Russia's strict, conscience-awakening, and humane literature, which had its best manifestation in the works of Tolstoy and Dostoyevsky. Although the West does not understand its spirit, seeing in it a kind of foolishness-for-Christ, this only proves that what is wise in the eyes of God is truly madness for the world.

From off the noisy streets of every city
You sweep the dirt—a useful task!
But is it right for priests to take
Your broom, and to abandon for your sake
Their altar, offering, vocation?
Not for the worries of the world,
Not for the coin, not for the sword,
But for the muse are we intended,
For prayer and harmonies transcendent.[76]

When the enemies of monasticism—due to an incorrect understanding of altruism—argue that it has no practical usefulness, why do they not remember these inspired words of the poet? Being the highest manifestation of spiritual culture, the monastic struggle (*podvig*) has no less a right to exist than poetry itself. It is not then surprising that poetry itself is seen as an idle and pointless diversion by the sons of this age, who have become accustomed to weigh everything on the limited scales of utilitarianism or simply crude materialism.

If a poet, "whose hearing graces the divine word, is filled with sorrow in this world's amusements, seeking ever to avoid society's noise,"[77] "if service to the muse can bear no earthly care,"[78] then how much less can the soul of a monk bear all these things, since it is completely directed toward the world above. The ascetic is, of course, much greater than the poet, for he is a chosen one of the heavens. His calling is to contemplate the Eternal Divinity face-to-face, as the "desired beauty," as St Basil the Great said, and to live in an atmosphere of exalted inspiration, "for prayers and harmonies transcendent," with which great monks have nourished and civilized the entire world.

Pushkin himself experienced the beneficial influence of a focused, solitary life that enlightens the soul and deepens the thought. Of this he spoke beautifully in his famous address to Chaadaev, describing the days of his exile in Bessarabia:

> Abandoning the noisy circle of those mindless boys,
> In exile I regretted nothing of those former joys.
> I sighed, and left behind still more of my delusions …
> And having torn apart those snares that bound me,
> My heart enjoys a new tranquility.
> In solitude my self-willed brilliance was taught
> To know both quiet industry and thirst for thought
> I rule my days; my mind's befriended order
> I learn restraint in deeper thought to calm disorder.[79]

No less vivid is his poetic description of his "desert of Mikhailovskoe," where he would often find refuge from the noise of society, and where the fountainheads of his creative genius would deepen as he remained alone with himself and his gift:

> I send you greetings, fair deserted corner,
> You haven of repose and work and inspiration …
> In this retreat from noisy shackles I am freed,
> A source of joy in truth I long to find,
> To deify the law with liberated mind …
> O oracles of ages, here I petition you.
> Here, in majestic isolation
> Your joyful voice I hear most true,
> You banish far the sullen sleep of indolence,
> Inflaming industry and love for work in me,
> And all your thoughts' creative excellence
> Bear fruit within, too deep to see.[80]

The silent desert has its own language of instruction, something well understood by a certain wise Englishman in a recent book called "The Wisdom of the Desert."

Is this not why ascetics left the world for caves and crevasses in the earth, to have a freed spirit, to find joy in truth, to hearken to eternal heavenly speech that becomes more easily heard in "majestic isolation."

All of creation there reveals itself to the eyes of the monk in the effulgence of eternal harmony, whose echo we hear in the inspired hymn placed into the mouth of John of Damascus by Aleksey Tolstoy:

> I sing your praises, forests green
> Valleys, fields, heights, rushing waters,
> I sing a song of praise to freedom
> And skies bedecked in deepest blue.

"Everything surrounding me," said a certain pilgrim who wrote a wonderful confession of his own heart, "appeared to me in a unique form. The trees, the grass, the birds, the earth, the air, the light— everything seemed to tell me that it exists for man, witnesses to the love of God for man. Everything prays, everything lifts up praise to

God." Although he leaves the world with his body, the monk does not separate himself from the world in his spirit, for "the monk is the one," said St Nilus of Sora, "who, though distant from all, remains in spiritual communion with all and in every person sees his own self."

If the world cannot recognize the true significance of monasticism, this is evidently only because this must be understood in a spiritual manner (1 Corinthians 2:14). Bacon doubtless understood well the importance of judging spiritually when he said, "the masses praise the lowest virtues, wonder at the middle virtues, and have no sense of the highest virtues."[81]

Monasticism, which strives to embody fully the ideal moral Christian life, is truly the salt of the earth, which can alone save the world from complete decomposition. It does not destroy anything truly human in people, but only elevates, purifies, and ennobles the human soul. It always reminds the world that God alone should be the goal of our desires and our foundation. However much true monastic spirit remains on earth (which may, of course, manifest itself even in the world), so much true spirituality, true religiosity, and true humanity remain here as well.

Every tree is recognized by its fruits. Secular people who visit the best of our coenobitic monasteries are often amazed at the order not only of the monks' inner spiritual culture of life, but the external beauty and order as well. How can you explain that monks, who are so distant from the world, so easily assimilate the latest technological and cultural innovations? Where do the talents come from in the middle of the desert? Where do those whose education rarely exceeds simple literacy find such subtle taste and wisdom? The answer to these questions in found in the very nature of true monastic life. Constant descent into the self refines the spiritual talents of a monk; prayer purifies and clarifies his thought and brings into harmony his reason, emotion, and will. It opens within him the sources of creativity inherent in every person. Faith, for which everything is possible, augments his natural gifts. Humility kills self-contentment, always a source of mental and moral stagnation, forcing the monk to move ever forward. Obedience turns his every work into a moral-ascetic labor, which makes him especially productive. The lack of a battle for a personal existence or any personal property whatsoever forces the monk to think always about the increase of the common treasury, from which every person may receive all that is necessary to satisfy daily needs. Finally, the general harmony of the inner and external life, as well as constant contemplation of the beauties of heaven, fosters in a monk a sense of the refined, with which he impresses all the works of his hands and even the nature surrounding him.

Seeing all these particularities of the inner lifestyle of the cenobitic monastery, one cannot help but admit that only in such a life, detached from the world, can we find an example of the highest social order on earth, the same kind of order that politicians and sociologists grasp at in vain.

Do not be a strict judge of those who teach with their words alone about great virtues, especially when they themselves are lazy to act according to their own teachings, for their insufficiency in deed is often made up for in the worth of their teaching. We have not all acquired everything in equal measure; some have a preponderance of words to the detriment of actions, which others make up for the lack of words with action.[82]

In these thoughts of St John of the Ladder we find a certain consolation for those who serve the word, if they do not themselves fulfill everything to which they call others. The teaching word is itself merited to them. Laboring for the sake of their brothers and neighbors to direct them along the correct path of life, they, by the strength of the intimate connection among all men, compensate their lack with the virtue of their word.

This thought, of course, cannot replace the eternal word of the Eternal Teacher: " ... whoever does and teaches them, he shall be called great in the kingdom of heaven" (Matthew 5:19). People whose deeds correspond to their words will always remain the best teachers of mankind.

Konstantin Leontiev, that aristocrat of the spirit primarily, hotly battled the democratization of society, its "reduction by mixing," seeing in this the sign of the fall and breakdown of culture at large. Gustave de Bon develops the same though in his book *The Scientific Foundation for the Philosophy of History*. In it, he writes, "the fall of a nation can been seen in a return to the external forms of collectivism. Civilization is on the wane when the individual is again allowed to 'graze with the herd.'"

The entire philosophy of Nicholas of Cusa is founded on his teaching of "wise ignorance" that leads one to the "super-rational" knowledge of true reality in general, and the absolute reality of God in particular. Unfortunately, today's people do not even have the wisdom "to recognize their own ignorance," as St Gregory the Theologian said.

We live in an age of counterfeits. They follow us everywhere. We are forced to see not only faux beauty, insincere speeches, hypocritical actions, but even sham authors. This is the true sign of our times. Such people are not ashamed to put their names to others' work, merely in order to gain for themselves a literary fame.

The life of a person is so short compared to the eternal requirements of his spirit that everyone is ready to exclaim on his death bed: "I was tasting a little honey with the end of the rod that was in my hand. Behold! I must die!" (1 Kingdoms 14:43).

One of the Greek philosophers, Themistocles, lived to be 107 years old. Feeling the approach of death, he said, according to St Jerome, "that he is sad to leave the world at a time when he had just begun to be intelligent."

"Glorious indeed is the world of God around us, but more glorious the world of God within us," said Longfellow. This world can be seen only with the purified mind and a heart pacified by grace. Whoever has this vision, according to Isaac the Syrian, "finds joy in seeing his own soul, and wonders at his own beauty, which is one hundred times brighter than the sun's light. This is Jerusalem and the Kingdom of God hidden within us, according to the word of the Lord."

The famous poet Gumilev, killed by revolution (as was André Chenier), said the following wonderful words in conversation with another writer:

"I do not understand how a person who lived through revolution can remain without God. That is, I don't mean 'searching for God' in the usual sense. What's there to search for when are overcome by him and feel ourselves every moment to be in His hand? It's too late. He Himself found us already."

Gumilev wrote these amazing lines as though they were his confession before death:

There is the world, there's God, they live forever,
While our own life is momentary, scant.
But man can fit all things within himself
As long as he believes in God and loves the world.[83]

"All human laws aspire to be divine law" (Heraclitus).

The saints' love for God always superseded all earthly attachments.

St Ignatius, already condemned to the slaughter, wrote in his epistle to the Romans: "I fear your love, lest you hinder me. Do nothing for me, except that I may be devoured for God …"

"I beg you, do not be unduly attached to me."

The spiritual greatness of a person is immeasurably greater than the weak vessel of his body. Each one of us, through his consciousness, fits within himself, as it were, the entire universe. "I lie here, rolled into a ball," we read in one place of Leonid Andreyev's writings, "fitting into a mere yard and a half of space, but my thought encompasses the world. I see with the eyes of all people. I hear with their ears."

But here a terrible moral danger lurks in wait for every person. By being able to grasp the whole world with his mind, he is ready to declare himself to be the lord of the universe, while in actual fact he is no more than a miserable speck of dust. Such a proud thought is the greatest temptation for all intellectuals and thinkers. Orbiting in the spheres of abstract thoughts, they believe themselves from this height to be a special spiritual race, called to direct and command others and to rule over the world.

This is typical for our reason; as the Apostle Paul says, "knowledge puffs up," leading us often into delusion, while "love edifies" in all things, even in the acquisition of knowledge (1 Corinthians 8:1).

Here I unwillingly call to mind these somewhat caustic, but justified words of the Serbian poet Shajkovich in his epic poem *The New Prophet*:

> In reason finds the devil lordship
> And leads us far from truth
> To the heart alone is given understanding
> Of eternal truth, goodness, and beauty.

When St Thekla wanted to follow her teacher the Apostle Paul, he forbade her, saying, "No one goes with a bride to the battlefield."

It is well known that the world, from bird's-eye view, seems to us much more beautiful than seen close up, when we are in direct contact with it. Goethe evidently wanted to express this thought in these lines: "Man finds great pleasure in a painting of that which irritates him in life."

St Augustine said, "our soul and body are like two mutually unhappy spouses with different personalities, living in constant conflict while together, but despairing when forced to part."

Queen Maria of Romania, who wrote a *Story of My Life* in three volumes—a reviewer considered it to be the "best book written by a person with royal blood in any country"—confesses to have encountered "truly miraculous ways of God, great and awesome," during the days of the recent war in the fates of Romania at large and her own life.

Concluding her work, she said that people end "happily ever after" only in fairy tales, especially after living through terrible misfortunes. In life it is usually otherwise, and the royal writer finished her biography with the words of Ecclesiastes, who knew everything about the sorrow of kings: " ... for God has given painful distraction to the sons of men to be occupied therewith. I beheld all the works done under the sun, and behold, all is vanity and is the choice of one's spirit" (Ecclesiastes 1:13–14).

The deeper it studies the life of the world, the closer modern biology comes, unwillingly, toward religion. Today's naturalists pay especial attention to two phenomena in nature—the law of necessity and the fact of the constant creative impulse of every separate organism.

"This law of necessity in nature, especially in the makeup of organisms, astounds every scientist," writes Professor Metalnikov in his paper "Science and Ethics." "It is as if some kind of reasoning power took part in the formation of each organism. Every minute part of the organism, every single organ plays a necessary and specific role in the functioning of the entire organism."

On the other hand, we see in nature an endless diversity of forms and variations.

"One can say without exaggeration that in nature there are no two completely similar forms, just there are no two exactly similar actions or manifestations of an organism. This individual creative element that is the source of these eternal variations is only a small part of the general universal creative principle, which we call evolution."

The spiritual nature of a living organism, without which such phenomena would be simply inexplicable, is "just as real as matter and its laws."

Thus, biology, using simply the scientific method, leads us to "an admission of the Creative Reason that directs the activity of man and beast."[84] Once again, true science speaks in unison with religion.

Some of the most brilliant and inspired passages of Carlyle's *On Heroes, Hero-worship, and the Heroic in History* are a panegyric for the writer and the book, which is an impression of the "soul" of ages past and which reveals "an era of miracles."

Together with Fichte, he is ready to consider the writer a prophet and even a "Priest, continually unfolding the Godlike to men. Men of Letters are a perpetual priesthood, from age to age, teaching man that a God is still present in their life; that all 'appearance,' whatsoever we see in the world, is but as a vesture for the 'Divine Idea of the Word', for 'that which lies at the bottom of Appearance.' He is the light of the world; the world's Priest; guiding it, like a sacred Pillar of Fire, in its dark pilgrimage though the waste of Time."[85]

In this way, the great Pushkin was always, as it were, ritualizing during moments of creativity, and he even called moments of inspiration "a feast of God," his poetry—"holy," and himself—"a priest"[86] or "a prophet."

O, if only all of today's writers understood their calling to be so profound and holy, if only they held the banner of their responsibility so high! Unfortunately, among them predominate those whose hearts are not touched by "the divine word." The same Fichte considered such to be "counterfeit writers" or "pathetic scribblers," consigning them to nonexistence. They fill the book market with their counterfeit or even rotten literature, which brings great harm to our society, forcing them to lose their familiarity with healthy intellectual food.

Met Anastasy is greeted by children on a pastoral visit in Serbia.

Met Anastasy addresses the people after blessing the memorial erected by Russian refugees over the graves of the soldiers of General Alexander Suvorov. Lindau / Bodensee, Germany, 1948.

PART II

Essays on Revolution

Frightful and inscrutable is the dark face of revolution. Examined from the external facets of its existence, it does not fit within normal historical patterns; therefore, it cannot be studied together with other historical facts. Its deep roots go far beyond the limits of space and time, as determined by Gustave le Bon, who considered it an irrational phenomenon, in which some sort of mystical dark forces take an active role.

Whatever might have seemed doubtful before, it all became completely obvious after the Russian Revolution.

In it everyone felt, as a certain contemporary writer expressed it, the ultimate incarnation of absolute evil in human form; in other words, here he saw the evident participation of the devil, the father of lies and ancient adversary of God, who strives to make man his subservient tool, antagonistic to God.

The ancient war of evil against good, of dark against light, and of Satan against God comprises the deepest moral foundation of revolution, its secret soul and most important goal. Everything else that usually characterizes it, such as political and social upheaval, bloody passions given free rein, *et cetera* is only the external result or the means of this war; they have the same relation to revolution as the hands on a clock to the hidden spring that moves them.

The process of revolution weaves its way through all of mankind's history.

The first act of this great drama occurred in the heights of heaven, when a revolt arose among the fleshless spirits against the Creator, and its epilogue is depicted in fiery colors on the pages of the Apocalypse.

Lucifer first lit the fires of revolution in the world. We read about this in the Book of Isaiah:

"How you are fallen from heaven, O Lucifer, who rose up in the morning! He who sends for the nations is crushed to the earth. For you said in your mind, 'I will ascend into heaven; I will place my throne above the stars of heaven. I will sit on a lofty mountain, on the lofty mountains toward the north. I will ascend above the clouds; I will be like the Most High'" (Isaiah 14:12–14). He attracted to his cause "a third of the stars of heaven," that is, of the heavenly hosts; Michael the Archangel with the other bodiless hosts against them stood against them and cast them out of heaven (Revelation 12:4, 7–9). The Word of God does not give us a detailed image of this heavenly war, which Milton tried to depict with the help of his poetic imagination in *Paradise Lost*. He expressed all the moments of this uprising using language typical of revolutionary upheaval:

Though changed in outward lustre, that fixed mind,
And high disdain from sense of injured merit,
That with the Mightiest raised me to contend,
And to the fierce contentions brought along
Innumerable force of Spirits armed,
That durst dislike his reign, and, me preferring,
His utmost power with adverse power opposed
In dubious battle on the plains of Heaven,
And shook his throne …

He lordly sits
Our envied sovereign, and his altar breathes
Ambrosial odors and ambrosial flowers,
Our servile offerings …

But he who reigns
Monarch in Heaven till then as one secure
Sat on his throne, upheld by old repute,
Consent or custom …

Farewell, happy fields,
Where joy for ever dwells! Hail, horrors! hail,
Infernal world! and thou, profoundest Hell,
Receive thy new possessor—one who brings
A mind not to be changed by place or time.[87]

Cast out of heaven for his defiance, Satan not only did not humble himself before the Creator, but became even more entrenched in his war against God. He tried to induce the first man to enter the war on the devil's side, to place him at odds with his Maker. Poisoned for all eternity by the venom of pride, which sounded in the words "you will be as gods," the descendants of Adam could no longer heal themselves from this dangerous disease. Satan invisibly incited this fatal spirit of self-assertiveness in man, inducing him to fight against his own Creator.

The building of the tower of Babel was the first open challenge that mankind dared to cast at heaven. Punished for their impudence, they still did not humble themselves.

All of mankind's subsequent history of the Old Testament world became a continuation of the same antagonism of man toward God, which even the chosen nation of Israel participated in, as we clearly see in the Bible and especially in the books of the prophets.

This passion for battling God continued in a hidden form even after the coming to earth of Christ the Saviour, who reunited mankind with God and gave man the chance to once again feel the joy of Divine sonship.

The appearance of humanism, which tried to lead man out of submission to Divine Authority in order to declare man independent and to secularize all of culture that had grown from Christian roots, announced the beginning of a new act in this drama of the ages.

Revolution always comes with the temptation of absolute freedom, even divine freedom, the same promise that we first heard in Eden: "You will be as gods." Revolution always finds sustenance in this undying delusion of mankind, for which mankind has always paid such a heavy price.

The spirit of humanistic freedom that even infiltrated the Catholic Church resulted in an earth-shattering revolution known as the Protestant Reformation. The fires of the Reformation soon ignited the first great political and social revolution in England. It carried within itself in latent form all the typical destructive characteristics of subsequent revolutions, but the religious source of this movement, the iron fist of Cromwell, and the good sense of the English people managed to calm this storm, without allowing it to develop to its logical end.

From that time, however, the social atmosphere of Europe was forever tainted with the infection of revolution.

Prepared by the hands of Voltaire, Rousseau, and the Encyclopedists, French soil ended up the most receptive for the seeds of revolution, and they blossomed fully by the end of the eighteenth century, having given birth to the Great French Revolution. The close genetic ties between this Revolution and the English Reformation cannot be doubted, but every nation, of course, gives its own particular incarnation to revolutionary ideals. In contrast to England, in France there was nothing to stem the growing social storm; quite the opposite, in fact. Everything helped its quick spread.

In the French Revolution, as in a mirror, the frivolous character of the French was reflected, their desire to strike a pose, their love for pretty gestures and wordplay, inspired by vainglory. All the heroes of this Revolution—even the most moderate and serious of them known as the Girondistes—remind one of actors standing before a large audience, who think only of what their contemporaries and descendants will say about them. They would indulge in orgies the night before executions, just to show their so-called greatness of spirit. Many of them tried even to strike a proper pose on the scaffold, which for them was the last stage in this world.

Not one of them thought about their responsibility before God, before history, or before their own conscience in this fateful time.

When society is in such a state, revolution becomes not a means, but an end in itself, an idol before whom an entire nation bows. Carried along by its own inertia, France, like a hurricane, was propelled ever forward and eventually became a horrifying mix of blasphemy, cruelty, blood, debauchery, and collective insanity, which the Revolution's leaders vainly tried to cover up with the loud slogan: *Liberty! Equality! Fraternity!* Alas, next to every appearance of this slogan a "holy guillotine" would be built, which eventually became an insatiable Moloch, to whom a countless multitude of innocents were brought as human sacrifice. Reading everywhere the words "brotherhood or death," Chamfort unwillingly exclaimed: "This is the brotherhood of Cain!" Soon the entire world understood this fateful truth, and if at first even the most serious minds—such as Kant and Goethe—watched the development of the Revolution with curiosity, soon all Europe could feel was revulsion and horror.

The French Revolution clearly showed the world that its striving was not limited merely by the toppling of the existing governmental and social order; it appropriated to itself a more widespread mission on a global scale, and first of all declared itself a self-sufficient First Principle, announcing a new revolutionary moral code, revolutionary justice system, etc. It rejected the eternal laws of the Creator, in order to bow down before human reason and make it alone the giver of life's laws. Robespierre, the incarnation of the bloodiest aspect of the Revolution, which reached its zenith under his leadership, was the first to understand, however, the complete madness of man's war against God and therefore once again attempted to decree the worship of an Absolute Being, making himself high priest.

However, this pathetic parody of religion could save neither him nor the Revolution. Like Saturn, the Revolution continued to mercilessly eat its own children, until the iron fist of Napoleon ripped out its stinger. However, the spirit of the Revolution did not die, even after its horrifying conflagration was quenched finally in France. It became the greatest temptation for mankind, which did not stop looking back at these bloody, fiery pages of French history, so fatefully attractive for so many people.

The widespread influence of French culture, which was long a force in European social life, aided the spread of revolutionary ideas even more. The Russian educated elite embraced them, especially after Russian officers brought them back dangling on the ends of their bayonets after the triumphant invasion of Paris.

Every revolution first appears in the mind and only gradually electrifies the different social classes, beginning often, ironically enough, with the highest. Its underground work continues until the authority of the government and the strongest social forces begin to weaken. Then, like an underwater stream, revolution loudly breaks through to the surface. This happened in Russia after the disasters of the Great War, when the broken and exhausted national organism was no longer able to counteract this stormy, destructive force that had long seethed underground.

The Russian Revolution is one of the most complicated events in human history. It was weaved together from the most divergent forces possible. Here is an element of emulation of the French Revolution, the ideas of which an entire generation of the intelligentsia was reared upon. Here is also an element of "messianism" among the Westernizers, who mercilessly condemned Russia's political and social order and who later were disillusioned in "bourgeois" Europe. Here is also the apotheosis of Russia proper to the Slavophils, who considered Russia to be a light for the world, the future place for an idealized universal brotherhood of man. Here we also see the ancient, insatiable hunger for the truth proper to the common people, as well as their desire for more land. Here is also the anarchy of thought, invading Russia thanks to the negative sermonizing of Tolstoy and various other decadent harbingers of the storm. Here is also the profound shock in the Russian soul inspired by the fiery personages of abysmal evil in Dostoyevsky's fiction. Here is the enormous energy inspired by the Great War that sought an outlet after Russia's disappointing losses. Here is also Russian maximalism in general, which is unable ever to stop halfway, but quickly becomes nihilism. Here is also an echo of the Time of Troubles, as well as the uprisings of Razinskii and Pugachev, when Russian revolutionary tendencies showed themselves to be senseless and merciless, the result of the Russian soul's stormy mood in times of extreme agitation. All these forces were mixed together with the leaven of foreign, materialistic

Marxism, resulting in an unexpected and explosive fermentation that turned the sun into darkness and the moon into blood, resulting in troubles and horrors everywhere, making Russia into a terrible shame for the whole world.

Our Russian Revolution, of course, has no fewer characteristically national traits than the French, but if we are to look into its secret soul, we will see the same global revolutionary processes that have merely entered a new stage of development.

The Russian Revolution is bolder than all preceding revolutions. It immediately presented itself with a global mission and a profoundly radical program. Its ideologues do not want to see in it merely a repetition of "classical forms," which always finish with a compromise of some sort. This revolution, from its inception, set for itself a goal to reject the old world completely and to create an absolutely new order of social life, with new ideals and new methods of bringing it into being. The Revolution's goal was not to turn to a new page of world history, but to completely sever the connection with world history, to create a new world with a new mankind, whose apotheosis would become the center of a new dogma. Using the principle that "the pathos of destruction is the pathos of creation," it attacked all the former political, social, and moral order of life with the wrath of a fury, desiring to raze the old world to the very ground.

Here we see the dilemma of archetypal Russian maximalism: "Everything, or nothing," or, even better: "Everything, or down with everything."

It is interesting to note that not only Nechaev—that "destructor" *par excellence*—but even idealistic Alexander Herzen foretasted with some kind of demonic sensuality this future picture of general mayhem that must follow any Russian revolution.

"Or do you not see," said he, "these new barbarians seeking to destroy? They are ready. They are like lava that heavily moves underground inside mountains. When their hour comes, Herculaneum and Pompeii will disappear, both their good and their evil, the righteous and the guilty will die next to each other ..."

"What will come of this blood, who knows? But whatever happens, it is enough that in this frenzy of madness, revenge, dissension, retribution, the world that oppressed the new man and prevented the incursion of the future world will be destroyed. And this is wonderful, and so I welcome chaos and destruction. May the future come!"

Alas! This prophecy was fulfilled in its entire horrifying power. The barbarians have come to fulfill their fateful mission, and everything has become embroiled in bloody chaos.

Everything that was considered exalted, holy, virtuous, or merely honorable, proper, cultured in human life—all this has been desecrated and defiled by their cruel hand, and the abomination of desolation has settled in all places.

In the frenzy of madness, revenge, and dissension, the good, the bad, the innocent, and the guilty were all destroyed together. Wine has been mixed with blood and a sea of human tears at this new feast of Herod. Never before has human dignity been desecrated so crudely and mercilessly, never before has man fallen so low or been so revolting in his bestial insolence, as in this dark epoch. "For the body—violence, for the soul—falsehood." This principle of Nechaev was fully embodied, having become the founding principle of Bolshevism.

Every revolution is a great temptation taken advantage of by the spirits of darkness in order to attract to themselves not only individuals, but even entire nations. In revolution, in greater or lesser form, the three temptations of Christ in the wilderness are repeated. In the Russian Revolution, these temptations have been more evident than any another revolution in history. The more is given to the Russian people, the higher their calling, the lower was their fall.

The first temptation with which Revolution approached the Russian people was the temptation of bread, that is, a kingdom of universal satiety, equal distribution of earthly goods among all people, a phantom of earthly paradise, where there will be no poor or needy. For the sake of this purely earthly goal, the Russian people must reject all eternal spiritual ideals, by which they lived for many centuries.

The second temptation called the Russian people to reject the path of gradual improvement of social life, founded on ascetic labor, in order to embrace a miraculous leap forward into the kingdom of freedom, equality, and brotherhood, by which Russia was supposed to amaze the entire world. The third—the most terrifying of all—is the call to reject God and to worship his ageless adversary Satan, the better to conquer all the kingdoms of the earth with his help.

Even simple common sense shows us how dangerous and phantasmagorical each of these temptations is in their essence, but revolutionary psychology consults with common sense less and less. The Russian man, with his characteristic tendency to maximalism, did not think of hurling himself into the abyss, like Empedocles into the crater of Etna, to pass for a god. No, in his madness, the Russian man dared to enter open warfare with God Himself and to worship—actually, not symbolically—Satan himself. Satan has so possessed the Russian man's soul that in the madness of the Revolution we saw true demonic possession, the same kind that we encounter so often in the Gospels.

It must be said that in the appearance and establishment of atheistic materialistic communism on Russian soil, there is a certain unique dialectic.

Our radical intelligentsia, having wandered from the Church, took with itself the exalted principles of love and co-suffering with their common brother, as well as the idea—connected with the previous ideals—of self-sacrifice, freedom, equality, and brotherhood.

From this moral material, they wanted to form a new social order on earth, but without a religious foundation. However, a purely humanistic worldview, as historical experience has proven, cannot be a solid foundation for human life, for it always seems to be, as it were, hanging in the air, somewhere between heaven and earth. The Bolsheviks understood this intuitively and, pulled down by the gravity of the earthly, decided to found their kingdom firmly on earth. They did not hesitate to throw away all the idealistic traditions and preconceptions of their predecessors, and instead boldly followed Karl Marx, laying under their communist edifice a foundation of materialism. Having plunged themselves fully into the earthly, they naturally found themselves in the power of the ruler of the earth, the prince of this age. Satan did not wait to declare for them, through their own oracles, a new law, which can be nothing else but total opposition to the Law given on Sinai and in the Gospel.

If in the past it had been said "I am the Lord your God, you shall have no other gods before Me," then this is the time when these other gods have appeared, and graven images are raised up and worshiped by the godless communists.

The fourth and fifth commandments—concerning honor given to feast days of the church and one's parents and elders—have been canceled completely.

Instead of the commandments "you shall not murder, steal, commit adultery, bear false witness, covet another's goods," new commandments, contrary to these, have appeared, turning what was previously vice and crime into revolutionary virtues.

It is not surprising that all the living shoots of life have dried up on the Russian land because of the hatred of those living on it, and Russia has become the vestibule of hell itself.

Satan did not even need to appear as an angel of light to fool the people. Instead, he has revealed his odious face—the face of a beast—making the entire world tremble. He led thousands of people to open war against the All-powerful Creator of the world. Militant atheism became the first principle of the Bolshevik program. The heavens must have truly been horrified at the vehement blasphemy rising up from the Russian land.

"Russia is the goal of revolution!" exclaimed Bakunin once. "Its greatest power will unfold there, and will there achieve its pinnacle. Exalted and brilliant will be the bloody and fiery constellation of revolution rising up above Moscow, becoming a guiding star for all of liberated mankind."

Truly, having gone consecutively through three stages of development in three European countries, the spirit of revolution, so it would seem, reached its pinnacle in Russia, manifested in a previously unseen satanically cruel atheism, in sadistic cruelty and horrifying amorality, while the constellation of the revolution, formed from a sea of blood and fire, did not illumine a tableau of earthly paradise, but a kingdom of slavery, hunger, and death, which has already devoured millions of innocents and turned the greater part of Russia into a desert. It could not have been otherwise. The path of Antichrist is everywhere made manifest by suffering and death.

Those who continue to idealize the revolution—this terrifying beast with bloody hands, face twisted with hatred and hellish laughter, eyes full of brazen shamelessness, with which it defiles all that is divine in man—despite all its horrors, should at the very least remember more often the characteristics of revolution as defined by its former ideologues: "Revolution is a barbaric form of progress," said the famous French socialist Jaurès, who wrote a twelve-volume history of the French Revolution. Even more eloquent is the denunciation of the aforementioned Bakunin, in a rare moment of spiritual illumination: "Blood revolutions, thanks to human stupidity, become sometimes necessary, but still they are an evil and a great misfortune not only for its victims, but also for the purity and fullness of that goal for which it is accomplished … Fate decrees that after mass killings, revolutionaries are forced to come to the depressing conclusion that they won nothing and with their own hands they prepared the triumph of reactionaries."

"O proud and holy liberty!" wrote Rousseau on April 30, 1791, in a letter to Empress Catherine II. "If pathetic mankind could come to know with what price you are bought and preserved, if people would only feel that your laws are less mutable than the worst tyranny, their weak souls, distracted by passions, would fear you one hundred times more than slavery, or they would run from you, terrified, as from a giant ready to crush them."

The Jacobin Carnot, having traveled the treacherous road of freedom during the French Revolution, only confirms Rousseau's condemnation, which was founded more on intuition than on actual experience: "Liberty teases man, but he never is able to taste it. Eternally extending his hand to this fruit, he will be struck down by death." If we will add Jeanne Roland's confession as she was being led to her execution past the statue of Liberty—"O Liberty! What crimes are committed in your name!"—then it will become understandable how dangerous is the temptation of unfettered liberty that Revolution has offered to mankind from the first days.

These "classical" witnesses to the true face of Revolution are echoed by many contemporary thinkers, such as Nikolai Berdyaev. "All great revolutions," he writes in his famous book *The Philosophy of Inequality*, "flow inexorably forward. All have been wrathful, angry, revengeful. In all revolutions the most radical faction has always prevailed, in all revolutions freedom has been rejected and the image man has been perverted. Revolution is not an idyll; revolution has never been beautiful or good; never have the better angels of human nature prevailed in revolution. All revolutions awoke the dark and evil side of man, the primordial Chaos. Never have revolutions been reasonable. Never have they brought joy and never have they given that liberation, of which their predecessors dreamed ... "

"Revolution is the doom of nations and a great calamity," he writes in another book, *A New Dark Age*.

There can be no doubt that every revolution takes the path of least resistance, that evil becomes strong in the world only when good weakens, that as with any other temptation, revolution bears within itself a cruel retribution for those whom it ensnares.

However, all this cannot give revolution even the smallest bit of moral justification. It cannot be examined as a providential historical Nemesis who exacts retribution on the government and society for sins of the past and who contains within itself the medicine for political and social diseases, for in this case the medicine is far more fatal than the disease itself. It bleeds the national organism dry for a long time, and sometimes destroys it outright. The suffering of hell will be the punishment for man's sins, but they will not purify sinners. The same can be said of the fires of revolution, which have the capacity to harden people in evil instead of improving them or softening their hearts. This phenomenon cannot be equated even to various natural disasters such as earthquakes and floods, which God allows for the instruction of mankind, for in revolutions human will acts, consciously striving to destroy and break apart the human soul, while God, of course, can never be an abettor of evil.

In its essence, revolution is a destructive principle (this is proven by the word itself, which means "explosion, perturbation, rebellion"). Together with good, it even partially destroys evil, but it cannot create life until it rejects itself, that is, its hellish essence. No one picks grapes from a blackthorn bush. No healthy fruit will grow from a rotten root. If the All-wise Provider can extract some good from it for us, this is, of course, not *thanks* to revolution, but *in spite of* it.

Revolution itself can only give off evil and catastrophe for mankind. This is why today many who formerly were ready to bow down to it as a goddess-liberator have now turned away in horror.

Having sobered up at the cost of bitter experience, they now warn others about the appealing temptation of revolution.

Summarizing "the profit and loss of war and revolution," the famous sociologist Professor Sorokin, having paid his own tithe, along with many other intellectuals, to the psychosis of revolution, finds that the profits do not cover the losses:

> This is why I react with skepticism to any joy and ecstasy—either naïve or refined—at the idea of revolution ... When I see many many workers genuinely dreaming of the coming of revolution, I tell them, "How sad it is that mankind has not learned the lessons of history." They are children playing with fire that will burn them and the working classes most of all. They will call up a storm that will spread death, murder, hunger, disease, devastation in their entire country. As a result, the common people will suffer the most ...
>
> The method of forced hunger and bloody violence by its nature gives nothing other than destruction. "The spirit of destruction is not the spirit of creation." This we have now all understood.
>
> Even if revolution had some positive results (which, alas, almost never happens), these fruits are not worth the "pure tear of a single child." People's lives become nothing more than bricks, their blood the cement holding them together, their suffering the plaster, horrors and bestiality the paint—this is the revolutionary

method of building the social edifice. Not one life, not the tears of one adult, but tens of thousands of children are laid down as the foundation of such an edifice. They are mercilessly choked, smothered, shot, killed by typhus, syphilis, cholera, scurvy, and other diseases. They soft bones are broken, not only their bodies, but their souls are twisted beyond recognition ... This is all too dear ... far too dear ... [88]

The most important positive achievement of any revolution consists in its self-rejection and in the graphic confirmation of the truth that *evolution is far greater than revolution*. Only evolution leads the world along the path of true progress. The catastrophe of revolution leaves behind itself such cultural ruins and such deep moral wounds that entire centuries cannot heal. Pushkin showed the true discernment of genius when he taught us, through the mouth of Grinev, in *The Captain's Daughter*:

"Young man, if these reminiscences come into your hands, remember that the best and most long-lasting changes are those that come from an improvement of one's way of life, without any violent disruptions."[89]

Another, no less important, breakthrough achieved by mankind after the revolution consists in the confirmation of the truth that religion is so deeply ingrained into the fabric of human nature that man cannot live without it, just as he cannot have an ambivalent attitude to it. Man can only either follow religion or persecute and hate it. Revolutionaries, especially the Bolsheviks, do not only try to destroy the existing religion, but also to replace it unnoticeably with another, created by themselves in their own image and likeness. By their own demonism, the Bolsheviks showed that "religious neutrality," as Berdyaev said, "does not exist, that the religion of the Living God is opposed only by the religion of the devil, that the religion of Christ is opposed only by the religion of Antichrist."

Having rejected the True God, they created for themselves false idols, to whom they truly gave almost divine characteristics. Lenin and Marx became for them the same thing that Mohammad is for the

Moslems. Their teaching is accepted not only as the only true teaching, but one that is completely infallible and eternal. It needs not a single reasonable justification and should be accepted on faith, as a religious dogma. "The teacher has spoken." This is enough for his word to become law for all time.

Thus is man. Having separated himself from God and having warred against Him, he does not stop seeking an infallible divine Authority. "Thus does the human soul commit adultery against God," said Blessed Augustine, "when it turns away from You, seeking outside You that which in complete purity can be found only by returning to You. Perversely do they emulate You when they turn away from You and raise themselves up in Your sight."

Revolution, as is well known, is born first of all in the soul of man. Who then brought forth the revolution of the Russian spirit, from which later came, like a chick from an egg, the greatest catastrophe of our days?

The Decembrists, whom the Bolsheviks consider their first ancestors in ideology?

Herzen, Bakunin, and especially Nechaev, who formed to its conclusion the ideal of communism and therefore are fairly called the harbingers of the Bolsheviks?

Or those prophets of the coming storm who appeared at the end of the nineteenth century and especially in the beginning of the twentieth, forming an anarchy of minds in politics and religions, in science, the arts, music, poetry?

All these factors were of course instrumental in the gradual decomposition of the Russian soul and all prepared a social psychology conducive to the appearance of the Russian Revolution, but the true spiritual reformers of their age, who created a huge commotion in almost all aspects of Russian life and culture, were two of the greatest Russian thinkers of the last century—Tolstoy and Dostoyevsky.

Having embodied in himself all the typical characteristics of the Russian nation, from its highest social classes to the lowest, being just as limitless, unfettered as the Russian people, having united within himself both a refined intellectual—with his self-criticism, spiritual wandering, and rationalism—and a Russian peasant or *muzhik*— with his attraction to the earth, hatred for the educated and rich classes, and the thirst, if not for a new heaven, then at least a new earth on which would rule truth—having always sought the truth and often battled it, Tolstoy fit within himself the echoes of all these thoughts and moods, and from this union came the first spark that lit the conflagration of the Russian Revolution.

He was for Russia a Rousseau and partly a Voltaire. Tolstoy considered himself to be a student of Rousseau, and even wore a small portrait of him, like a holy relic, around his neck. As for Voltaire, at first glance there seems to be little spiritual affinity between them. However, Tolstoy was doubtless a "Voltairian" in practice, and his cutting jibes against the Church had no less an influence of Russian society than the sarcasm of Voltaire, directed at the Catholicism of his time.

If we are told that Tolstoy sought to bring a Christian foundation to the culture of his time, we must answer that the tombstone of Voltaire has, among his many achievements, the following words: "He battled atheists." This was no exaggeration, since he was a Deist, and certainly not an atheist. It is also doubtless that Tolstoy's character and convictions were directed violently against evil; therefore, he rejected the courts, the entire government apparatus, and he especially hated the French Revolution, calling it a "big" revolution, but not a "great" one. He was also against all attempts in Russia to change the existing political and social order by revolutionary means, of which he openly spoke to both students and members of the working class. His calls to transform social interactions along the principles of Christian brotherhood and love, of course, had nothing in common with the hatred of man typical of the Bolsheviks. However, when he began to criticize the government, society, and culture of his time, his pen was so full of the vitriol of protest, anger, and mockery that he unwillingly became the ally of the revolutionaries.

"Mockery," Spencer said, "has always been an agent of revolution. All establishments that have lost their roots in faith and the respect of the people become cursed to failure." The many years of Tolstoy's propaganda against much that was close and holy to the Russian heart, together with his attempt to simplify his manner of living, could not pass by without affecting the national soul, gradually subverting all the foundational elements of Russian life. He truly overturned, as his son Lev Lvovich said, from top to bottom the consciousness of the Russian people and created a new Russia. With his sharp and profound literary plough, he furrowed Russia's soil for the seed of revolution, which, again according to L.L. Tolstoy, was "prepared and morally sanctioned by him."

It is much harder to establish and follow the influence on the appearance and development of the Russian Revolution that Dostoyevsky's works had. He, of course, had nothing in common with Rousseau, Voltaire, or the Encyclopedists. To many even the way I phrase the question of any supposed connection of the Revolution with the literary works of Dostoyevsky will be nothing short of blasphemy. Our social attitude has long ago canonized this great writer. All have become accustomed to bow down reverently before the brilliant prophetic vision of Dostoyevsky, who described the face of revolution—bloody, cruel, and atheistic in its essence—before it happened.

In his novels *Devils* and *The Brothers Karamazov*, as in a mirror, with incredible accuracy, Dostoyevsky reflects that mass demonization, that satanic possession and pride that socialism brought to Russia. But by depicting with such incredible vividness this imminent Kingdom of Ham, or, better yet, Antichrist himself, Dostoyevsky did not reveal, however, any of the epic passionlessness of the great ascetics, nor that angry tone or inner suffering that comes from the pen of some of Russia's writers (such as Pushkin and Lermontov) when they merely come into contact with the snares of Satan manifesting themselves in the life of the world. That and the other feeling, so to speak, ensure the reader against being tempted by evil, which is always inherent to our perverted nature.

Dostoyevsky clearly sees the demonic character of the coming revolution and its masterminds, but the brush with which he paints these men, together with his passionate character (he himself admitted that he liked to "push the envelope," so to speak) both led him farther than was necessary for his goal of morally instructing society and farther even than he himself wanted. Thanks to the earth-shattering power of his dramatic talent, he reveals evil to us with blinding clarity, with nothing to cover it, and he so fully embodies himself in his anti-heroes, as though he becomes spiritually one with them, that this feeling unwillingly passes on to the reader. The same thing happened with these personages as what happened to the eyes of the portrait in Gogol's eponymous story. In these eyes is laid some kind of magic power, which simultaneously attracts and repels the human soul. It is never safe for a mortal to touch the tree of the knowledge of good and evil, nor to approach the abyss of hell. The latter will always attract to itself, and it then burns the curious one with its fiery breath. Like Dante, Dostoyevsky leads the reader through the inferno and forces him sometimes to put the fiery words of his books down, so that the reader can rest from that darkness into which he sometimes casts us.

K. Zaitsev had the right to say, "sometimes it even seems that Satan speaks through Dostoyevsky's mouth." Unfortunately, his idealized positive characters do not give enough of a counterbalance. Manifestations of the exalted aspects of the human spirit, for such a natural talent as Dostoevsky was, are always much more difficult to realize in literary form than the satanic depths of evil. It would not be a sin against the truth or against the great writer to say that the meek personality of Elder Zosima or Alyosha Karamazov is in no way capable of outshining the vivid characterization of Ivan Karamazov, with his self-assertive pride, who shines before us with some kind of baleful phosphorescence. His proud sufferings do not elicit any compassion from us, for even Satan is a "martyr" of his own freedom.

With his sometimes cruel pen, Dostoyevsky, as with a scalpel, cut into the soft Russian heart, and, shaking it to its very core, threw it out of spiritual balance. He showed the impressionable Russian society an attractive personage who stands beyond good and evil, and in this way he came into contact, as is well known, with Nietzsche. It is not by accident that Nietzsche felt some affinity to the writings of Dostoyevsky, and even said that Dostoyevsky was the only profound psychologist, from whom he could take something for himself. Developing in all his works his favorite idea of the two extremes that battle in the depths of the Russian heart, both of which have, so to speak, equal rights to existence, since man is ultimately a free being, Dostoyevsky indirectly gave the revolution if not a moral, then at least a psychological justification.

In this sense, both bitter and sweet water flows from his works. There is no doubt that in his personal life he overcame the forces of evil, but he does not pass on this feeling to others, and he does not give the ultimate and spectacular victorious power to the good. Instead, he allows the reader himself to make the choice between good and evil, overestimating the ability of man to make the correct choice, since he has been polluted by sin.

Therefore, he gave birth, so to speak, to two generations of people. The first follow him to the end through the ascetical labor of faith, love, and humility, all the way to the gates of paradise lost. The second stop, like Lot's wife, along the way and look back at Sodom and Gomorrah, incapable of overcoming their inner attraction to temptation.

From this second generation came an entire series of young writers who absorbed first of all Ivan Karamazov's rebellion and brought it into the common people, with the desire to "revolutionize" them. There is no doubt that Dostoyevsky himself would have angrily rejected these so-called ideological descendants of his; however, they would have been right to say that they took from his works all the material they needed for their destructive literary work.

Since great minds unwillingly cast a large shadow into the future, did not the opposite occur of Dostoyevsky's intention? Did not Dostoyevsky himself, by the vivid realization of the spirit and form of the coming revolution, help the Bolsheviks actualize their ideal, to give it a concreteness, a horrid fervency, a self-styled adherence to principle? Perhaps the revolution happened as Dostoyevsky foresaw not only because he had insight into its true essence, but because he partially predetermined its form by the power of psychological suggestion coming from his realistic, creative genius, having forgotten the command of Gogol, according to whom every creative work must bring to the human soul solace and reconciliation, not confusion and division. In any case, this entire question, despite its tragic nature, requires a more thorough, thoughtful, and objective analysis. This will be the responsibility of future generations.

The Russian Church was fated to pass through two temptations during the revolution: a temptation by power and might, then later a temptation of abasement and suffering.

When the throne of the tsars fell to the revolution, when local government authority failed, when the army lost its power, political parties weakened, and other social organizations collapsed, then among these ruins of the previously mighty Russian land, the only edifice left standing was the majestic Church, having preserved the entire power of its moral authority and having manifested to all an integral organism when once again it was led by a Patriarch of all Russia. Patriarch Tikhon became a living symbol of the oneness of the Russian land, as well as a true leader, as was Patriarch Hermogen during the Time of Troubles. Unwillingly, the eyes of all who desired the salvation of Russia were turned toward him. The hopes, not only of those who would restore the old order, but even those of more left-leaning tendencies who so often reproached the Church for its close ties with government, hinged on the authority of this man.

Seeing that the mere word of Patriarch Tikhon could summon hundred of thousands of people for triumphant processions with the cross or all-Russian commemoration services in Moscow (especially after a famous miracle of an icon of St Nicholas, located on the gates of St Nicholas in the Kremlin), and that the residents of Petrograd gave him a king's welcome, even left-leaning liberals understood his importance for this historical moment and approached him countless times with suggestions that he use his authority to inspire the popular masses against the still-shaky authority of the Bolsheviks.

At the same time, both our former allies and our enemies (the Germans) tried to take advantage of his name and influence. They both hoped to attract the Russian army to their own cause, since at that time the Russian army still seemed capable of turning the tide of the Great War to whatever side it chose to fight on.

The temptation for the Russian Church was very great. It was all the more tempting to take the sword of Caesar, since the people and history itself seemed to offer it to the Church. However, if it had decided to take this step, to redden its pure robes with human blood, the Church would have to take heavy responsibility for the civil war that was just beginning, and its authority would have been compromised for all time.

Bowing down to its own inner feeling and even more to the commandments of the Orthodox faith, which has from the beginning avoided all clericalism and attractions of worldly power, the Patriarch, and with him the entire Council of the Russian Church, refused to go along such a dangerous path, but on the other hand it used all its authority to wield a spiritual sword to fight off the ascendant atheistic power. The Church openly accused and unmasked the communists in official conciliar documents, sermons, even in the Kremlin itself (at the Patriarch's enthronement), as well as those avenues in the press that still remained available. Especially majestic and stern was the voice of the Patriarch Tikhon, who boldly and with great power of spirit called down spiritual punishment on the enslavers and degraders of the Russian Land.

His historic anathemas on the atheists, which fully unmasked the amoral, debauched essence of the new authority, cannot be read without inner trepidation. They will forever witness in defense of the Russian Church, which found its worthy manner of action and a corresponding language in such a critical moment for Russian history.

When the communist power later found firm footing, it openly declared war on the Church. However, the Church was not afraid of this new temptation, the opposite of the previous one, and met persecution by the Soviet government with majestic calm and dignity.

Many bishops, priests, and monks, as well as faithful laypeople, met their sufferings with something akin to joy and enthusiasm, worthy of the first Christians. Hundreds of hieromartyrs, martyrs, and confessors, whose number continues to increase, proved to the entire world the indestructible might of the faith of Christianity, and persecutions once again became the "seed of the Church," as Tertullian so profoundly wrote.

If, however, a small number of those weak in faith, who could not withstand this great temptation, was revealed next to these heroes of the spirit, then we must remember the same was true in the first centuries of Christianity. It is enough to read the bitter rebuke of St Cyprian of Carthage to those who denied the faith to be convinced of this.

Besides the weakness of human nature in general, a mitigating circumstance for the Russian people can be the fact that they have been burning in these testing fires already many years, during which religious persecutions, masquerading as political reprisals, have not ceased almost for a single moment.

Compared to this, even the years of the French Revolution seem short. As for the early Church, even though those persecutions lasted, all told, almost three centuries, the persecutions were never so protracted and sustained as today. Thanks to the frequent change of emperors, the politics of the Roman authority with reference to Christianity often changed as well. From time to time, God in His mercy sent humane rulers, under whose reign Christians could rest for a time from pagan persecutions, to be strengthened in spirit for new persecutions to come.

It seems hardly necessary to add that the common spirit of the life of the first Christians, who were on fire with holy zeal for their faith and who thirsted to see as quickly as possible the revelation of the Kingdom of Christ, was much more conducive to the brave bearing of suffering for the sake of faith than this weak and faithless age.

Finally, Orthodox Russia, during its thousand-year history, never saw a systematic persecution of religion, and so was not sufficiently experienced to battle the enemies of the Church and to uncover the snares of Satan's slaves, who in these days use all possible means of atheistic propaganda and the most refined spiritual temptations and tortures to subvert the faithful from the path of the truth.

"For what reason does the Russian nation and the Russian Church suffer? Why does God not cut down the evil that seems to triumph everywhere over good?" Many ask this question now.

This question, if looked at in a global sense, has worried mankind since ancient times.

St Ignatius's Brianchaninov's *Otechnik*[90] has the following story about Anthony the Great. He was once brought to great perplexity by the profundity of the economy of salvation and God's judgment. Having prayed, he said, "Lord, why do some people reach old age and decrepitude, while others die as children? Why are some poor, and some rich? Why do tyrants and evil men prosper and gather earthly benefits, while the righteous are oppressed by poverty and need?"

He was long occupied with these thoughts and then heard a voice: "Anthony, be vigilant to yourself and do not seek to plumb the depth of God's judgments, for this is harmful for your soul."

The innocent sufferer Job, who wanted to defend himself before God, once heard a similar answer in the storm and whirlwind. "Who is this who hides counsel from Me, and holds words in his heart and thinks to conceal them from Me? Gird your waist like a man; I will question you, and you shall answer Me. ... Do you not reject my judgment? Do you think I have dealt with you in any other way than might appear to you to be righteous? Have you an arm like the Lord's? Or can you thunder with a voice like His?" (Job 38:2–3, 40:8–9).

Even the friends of God could not understand the judgments of God's Providence in the history of the world. Even the King and Prophet David's "steps had well-nigh slipped" (Psalm 72:2), as he considered this mystery. It also disturbed the heart of Patriarch Abraham, when he appealed to God's mercy, seeing the condemnation of Sodom and Gomorrah, as well as the Prophets Jonah and Elijah, who demanded that God punish the unrighteous. The Preacher in Ecclesiastes, seeing that "the race is not to the swift, nor the battle to the strong, nor bread to the wise, nor wealth to men of understanding" (Ecclesiastes 9:11).

Righteous men have known that "His [God's] eye is too pure to see evil," and they were perplexed: "Why then do You ... keep silence when the ungodly swallow up the just?" (Habakkuk 1:13). The prophet Jeremiah was even so bold to try to struggle with the very Lord and Provider of the world, to Whom he brought a grievance for His own judgments on this earth: "O Lord, You are righteous, that I may plead my case with You, to speak to You concerning judgments. Why does the way of the ungodly prosper, and all who deal treacherously flourish? You planted them, and they took root. They bear children and are fruitful" (Jeremiah 12:1–2).

The Lord never revealed the fullness of His dispensation for the world to anyone, not because He did not want to, but because people would not be able to understand it due to the narrowness of their view of the world, which cannot comprehend the vast richness of the wisdom and reason of God as revealed in the Divine mastery of the world. In order to understand the paths of God's providence in history, one must understand fully the state of the current world, as well as the past and future fates of the universe, for all this is indissolubly connected in the one plan of Divine economy. Such a breadth of vision is, of course, inaccessible to man, in the same way that a child cannot understand the thought and intention of his father when he tries to work everything out for his benefit, and in such a way that his benefit will also coincide with what is good for the whole family.

Only after the fulfillment of the ages, when the end of the world will come and the Kingdom of Christ will be revealed, only then will all the mysterious judgments of God be justified, before which all of redeemed mankind will reverently bow down, giving Him "blessing and glory and wisdom," as we read in the Revelation 7:12. Until that time comes, God will only reveal to people, from time to time, in very small measure, and for only exceptional circumstances, His all-wise will, leading individual nations and the whole world along this or that historical path. Either He reveals His will directly to His chosen ones, with whom He speaks as though face to face, or He reveals it in the march of world events, directed by His right hand.

Zealous for the sake of God's glory, when He is vilified by the sons of this age, righteous men often ask why the All-powerful God does not immediately take His revenge on the proud and unrighteous who rise up against His eternal and all-powerful dominion. God answers them through the Prophet Hosea: "For I am God and not man; the Holy One among you" (Hosea 11:9). God is too mighty, Chrysostom says, to take revenge on someone immediately. At the same time, He is so far above the world that He cannot be offended or even touched by the tongue of vain babblers. Every blasphemer is truly like a dog that barks at the moon.

"Assume now majesty and power, and clothe yourself with glory and honor. Send forth messengers with wrath and humble every insolent man" (Job 40:10–11). Only human zeal can speak such words, because it is often impatient only because it is not balanced with love, the very essence of God's nature. God's mercy often, as it were, holds back His punishment for a time. "The Lord is not slack concerning His promise, as some count slackness, but is longsuffering toward us, not willing that any should perish but that all should come to repentance" (2 Peter 3:9).

"But you are merciful to all, for You can do all things; and you overlook the sins of men … You spare all things, because they are Yours" (Wisdom of Solomon 11:23, 26). His mercy and justice do not want to destroy the wheat along with the tares that have become intertwined even at the level of the roots. He is ready to have mercy on condemned Sodom and Gomorrah for the sake of ten righteous men, lest those ten be destroyed together with the unrighteous. He did not want to destroy Nineveh for the sake of 120,000 innocent children and even for the sake of the dumb beasts who would have been destroyed together with the sinful (Jonah 4:11). The measure of time itself is completely different for man and eternal God. "For a thousand years before Thine eyes, O Lord, are but as yesterday when it is past, and as a watch in the night" (Psalm 89:5). Divine Providence has "ordered all things by measure, number, and weight" (Wisdom of Solomon 11:20). For God, everything has its time and its proper time and duration.

> When he opened the fifth seal, I saw under the altar the souls of those who had been slain for the word of God and for the testimony which they held. And they cried with a loud voice, saying, "How long, O Lord, holy and true, until You judge and avenge our blood on those who dwell on the earth?" Then a white robe was given to each of them; and it was said to them that they should rest a little while longer, until both the number of their follow servants and their brethren, who would be killed as they were, was completed. (Revelation 6:9–11)

No one knows, of course, when this number will be completed.

Sometimes the Lord waits for evil to reveal itself completely, so that, having uncovered its true nature, it would begin to repel the hearts of men. He also tests the righteous man seven-fold, in order to reveal his spiritual beauty before the whole world and to increase his reward. Therefore, "He who is unjust, let him be unjust still; he who is righteous, let him be righteous still ... And behold, I am coming quickly, and My reward is with Me, to give to every one according to his work" (Revelation 22:11, 12).

If the righteous man burns even the smallest sins, universal to human nature, away in the fires of testing, then God allows the unrighteous to take temporary advantage of his prosperity so that he will also receive his reward for those scintillas of good accomplished during his life. The Just Judge does not want to remain a debtor, even to sinners. They do not know, of course, that He in this case is acting as a physician with the terminally ill, allowing His patients to allow themselves those joys that they cannot hope for in the future. Blessed Augustine with great eloquence and conviction reveals this thought in the passages concerning the fall of Rome in his *City of God*, which, as is well known, is the first attempt at a philosophy of history. The prosperity of those convicted to perdition is no more than a phantom, no more than smoke, and so it should not inspire envy in anyone, but rather should inspire bitter sorrow at their lot, for the Divine word is inviolable. "I shall repay on the day of vengeance" (Deuteronomy 32:35). "In a time of my reckoning, I shall judge according unto right" (Psalm 74:3). " … This I will begin, and I will finish it" (1 Kingdoms 3:12).

"Fret not thyself because of the wicked, neither be thou envious against them that do unlawfulness, for they shall soon wither like the grass, and quickly fall away even as the green herb" (Psalm 36:1–2).

"Weep over the sinner," one of the Fathers of the Church tells us, "who prospers in all things, for over his head hangs the sword of Divine justice."

As the Lord finds it necessary, He reveals His judgment over evil here on earth, as though He were answering mankind's plea: " … let me see Your vengeance on them, for I have revealed my righteous plea to You" (Jeremiah 11:19).

Thus, He poured forth His wrath on the evil deicide [a killer of a god], on those tools of the dark realm, who raised the God-Man up on the Cross.

Judas—the first of them—himself understood that after the crime he had perpetrated, he should no longer burden and defile the earth with his further existence upon it, and he condemned himself when, having cast away the hated pieces of silver—that price of the blood of the Master—went and hanged himself, and "falling headlong, he burst open in the middle and his entrails gushed out" (Acts 1:18).

The chief priests, scribes, and Pharisees—these people with seared consciences, striving by any means to condemn the Saviour of the world to death—experienced the bitterness not only of seeing the falling apart of their evil plots when Christ the Saviour rose from the dead and His teaching began to victoriously spread all over the world, but also of seeing (some in person, some through their children) the terrible days of Jerusalem's destruction. They were fated to experience calamities so terrible, they would never be repeated in human history.

Torn apart by hunger that forced mothers to eat their own children, burdened by the fraternal bloodshed and violence of the zealots, oppressed by terrifying foreboding, the residents of besieged Jerusalem endured indescribable sufferings, according to the writings of Joseph Flavius. When the hardened Roman soldiers finally broke into the city, they mercilessly began to slaughter everyone, no matter what the age or gender, and the hills surrounding Jerusalem were darkened, according to contemporary accounts, with the multitude of crosses on which hung those (or the descendants of those) who vehemently cried out to Pilate: "Crucify, crucify Him!"

Even the weak-willed judge, who had it in his power to save the Innocent One, whose innocence he himself admitted before the Jews, but sacrificed Him for the sake of friendship with Caesar, did not escape divine retribution. Vainly did he wash his hands before the people as a sign of his non-involvement in the committed evildoing. His hands were still bloodied with the blood of the innocent Sufferer, blood that the waters of the entire Jordan would not be able to wash off. He was also called to account for the shedding of this blood. Not long did he retain the goodwill of his Caesar. Denounced by the Jews for a different reason, he was removed from his post eight years after the Crucifixion and exiled to Vienna, where he committed suicide, like Judas the traitor.

The history of the Church, which is a continuation of the history of the life of its Founder, is full of similar examples. Even in our days, we see many miraculous events, when the Hand of God visibly casts down the proud, to give comfort to the righteous and to make evident to all that " ... verily there is a God that judgeth them on earth" (Psalm 57:12).

Nothing so painfully pierces the hearts of the faithful as open blasphemy and mockery of holy things, which God only allows when people become unworthy of those signs of His visible presence among them. For He himself revealed this to Solomon immediately after the consecration of the first true Temple on this earth:

If you or your sons turn from Me and do not keep My commandments and My statutes Moses set before you, but go and serve other gods and worship them, then I will cut off Israel from the land I gave them. I will cast from My sight this house which I made holy by My name. Israel will be destroyed, and will become but prattle among the peoples. As for this exalted house, everyone who passes by it will be astonished, and will hiss and say, "Why did the Lord do this to this land to this house?" Then they will answer, "Because they forsook the Lord their God, who brought their fathers out of the land of Egypt, out of the house of bondage, and thy embraced other gods and worshiped and served them. That is why the Lord brought all this calamity on them." (3 Kingdoms 9:6–9)

In this manner, God deprives His holy places of His presence and patronage only after the people themselves have left them and become indifferent to them.

"Let Us leave this place," said a voice in the Temple of Jerusalem, when it was condemned to destruction for the iniquity of the Jewish nation.

All these passages from the Word of God concerning God's providence acting in the world, and concerning human suffering, must be constantly in our minds especially now when we are ready to fall into depression at the appearance of evil's triumph everywhere. It is as if God has covered His face with a cloud, as the Prophet David said, to prevent our prayer from reaching Him (Psalm 9:32 (LXX)).

Here we must also add that revolution—that primary cause of our misfortune, fitting within itself fire, the sword, hunger, fratricidal war—cannot be fully equated with natural disasters or even with war. If those latter can occur suddenly and completely contrary to our will, revolution never occurs without the will and desire of the nation.

The nation either actively supports it or merely accepts it as an established fact, without standing up to it. Society can prevent its appearance and even stop its development in its very beginnings, if only it would desire to do so. But there is a fateful moment, when an entire nation decides, "if by blood, then by blood, if by chaos, then by chaos," and throwing down the gauntlet to fate frivolously leaps into the abyss. Knowing well enough that even the worst government is better than anarchy, the nation still, in a fury of impatience or madness, tears down with its own hands the last dam holding back the dark powers that threaten organized human life, and chaos bursts onto the stage of social life, inundating it like a flood. From that moment, human will is already powerless to battle this force that bears it forward on its stormy waves. Those who are the first to shake the foundations of government are the first to perish under its collapsing ruins. Slowly growing, this conflagration will not end until the entire country is reduced to ashes.

Thus, even the mere appearance of revolution is an act of profound moral collapse in a society that requires redemption and that carries within itself the most necessary retribution, in accordance with the famous axiom: "Your sin is your torment."

The masses of the Russian nation had a completely different attitude to the Revolution than did the French.

Our nation did not sanction the execution of its monarch, which occurred completely without the people's knowledge, and it can be said without exaggeration that this act was contrary to the will of the people. It was no accident that the murderers of our Tsar Martyr tried to hide his murder from the people for a long time. The Russian people, in general, accepted the Revolution half-consciously, since it was the work not of its mind and will, but of its temperament, as Bunin described very well in his *Life of Arseniev*:

"Oh, this eternal Russian need for a feast! How sensitive we are to it, how we thirst to be filled with life, not merely with pleasure, but truly fullness of life. Thus we are drawn to the buzz, to drunkenness! How boring is daily life and regularity of work … Was not this ancient reverie of rivers flowing with milk, of unfettered will, of feasting one of the most important reasons for the Russian Revolution?"[91]

Blok also considers this drunken carousal typical of the expansive Russian nature in his description of the revolution in his famous work *Twelve*. However, this drunken riot ended up too prolonged and dangerous. It resulted in the Russian man's *delirium tremens* and demonic hallucination. Such drunkenness cannot pass without a terrible shock to the national organism. The entire nation will feel the pain and suffering of becoming sober.

However, the state of drunkenness in which this or that crime is perpetrated cannot justify the crime. In the codified laws of some nations, it is even considered an aggravating circumstance. Even considering all the unique characteristics of our revolution, we cannot consider ourselves to be free of guilt, something so beautifully expressed by Metropolitan Philaret in answer to Pushkin's self-justifying poetic epistle:

> With my own self-willed power
> I called on evil from the depths
> Myself immersed my soul with passions,
> My mind with doubts discomfited.

If we called down this horrible disease on ourselves, then it depends first of all on us to be healed from it and its consequences.

The national organism must expel from itself the poison of Bolshevism, which is harmful equally in large or small doses. We must not merely reject it, but we must come to hate it and be revolted at its falseness. But the Russian people, corrupted by revolution, cannot be reeducated merely by words, no matter how beautifully uttered, nor with new political or social programs in opposition to Soviet communism with its dictatorship of the proletariat.

The kingdom of Satan cannot be destroyed with such weapons alone. "This kind does not go out except by prayer and fasting" (Matthew 17:21), that is, only by religious and moral ascetic labors (*podvig*).

The Revolution has perverted everything, beginning with the very idea that should be the foundation of any human society.

The famous slogan of the French Revolution—"liberty, equality, and fraternity," which is partially taken from the Gospels—is missing a fourth member: love. Only this virtue could crown, like a cupola, this triad, which without love lacks the inner wholeness needed to bring them to life and fruition. But the word "love" does not fit in the heart of a revolutionary, because it only feeds on hatred. For the leaders of the French Revolution, the idea of love was just as abhorrent as it is for Lenin, who wanted to completely eradicate the word "love" from the revolutionary lexicon. This is the source of all the internal contradictions of the Revolution, the most important of which is the fact that the attempt for universal equality destroys liberty.

"Liberty must be instituted by force," Marat triumphantly declared, and by doing so signed his own death warrant, "and it is necessary to establish a despotism of freedom, in order to crush the despotism of tyrants."

One of his fellow-thinkers, Madame Julienne, only brought this chain of logic to its conclusion when she said, "If you want an end, you must also want the means. To hell with barbaric humaneness!"

The Bolsheviks signed their names to this declaration with the blood of their countless innocent victims.

They made class warfare and animosity into a first principle, and it will take all the power and fire of true Christian brotherly love, woven into the fabric of social life, to counteract it.

We must reestablish "barbaric humaneness" and once again place it as the foundation for human interaction. At the same time, we must organize all the creative forces of the nation around the Church, in order to overcome the evil organized by the communists, which will long make itself felt on Russian soil. Instead of an "international," we must once again proclaim the idea of universal brotherhood in Christ.

In the battle with evil, we must sometimes learn from our adversaries, for the sons of this age are wiser than the sons of the kingdom in this age.

One American asked Lenin, "What is the source of the Bolsheviks' power?"

"What is the source of our power?" countered Lenin sarcastically, "You are asking this, you representative of the bourgeoisie?" His voice was full of ridicule. "I will tell you. Our power lies in your weakness, in your inability to organize yourselves and act, in your personal and class egotism, in your dissent and in your lack of courage. This is the source of our power."

In these cutting words is revealed the unfortunate truth that destructive elements in a society are usually more active and better organized than the conservative elements that uphold the social order, and so evil is capable of a show of great force, which in actual reality is nothing but a feint.

Lucifer lied to Cain in Byron's eponymous play, when in answer to Cain's question: "Are you happy?" he answered, "We are mighty."

This might is a mirage and cannot stand before the eternal and indestructible power of the Cross of Christ.

If the Russian people once again take up this spiritual weapon, then it will forever defeat the temptation of Bolshevism, and our suffering motherland, after its baptism by fire, will rise up again in new strength and glory, in order to accomplish its exalted historic mission—to become the chosen domain of Christ and a bastion of Orthodoxy, Holy Russia in truth.

"But Russia is still only a field sowed with dry bones. Will these bones arise, and if they will, when?" This question, full of sorrowful confusion, is asked by man who would like to see the quick resurrection of Russia. "O Lord God, You alone know this." This is the only answer possible. No one will dare to foretell the future, but we are duty-bound to prepare it.

Our irrevocable moral duty is to work for tomorrow (even if we ourselves never live to see it) and not to despair, believing in the final triumph of good over evil and in the victory of Christ over Antichrist.

Human history is full of contradictions and riddles. As difficult as this was to foretell, it is nonetheless true that the ideological ancestor of communism, even in its most radical forms, was the most humane of philosophers, the idealist Plato. He theoretically even anticipated the Bolsheviks by allowing, for example, the possibility of euthanizing all people over fourteen years of age, in order to forever rid his ideal Republic from a generation of elders and to pour new wine into old wineskins.

It is remarkable that all great revolutions repeat no sooner than a century apart, as though such a passage of time is necessary to store up the necessary revolutionary energy and also to forget the horrors of the previous catastrophe.

They are all similar to each other not only according to the law of emulation, which is typical of all mass movements, but also in the oneness of the spirit moving them. The same causes always produce the same results.

Other than these, universally known revolutions, there was a whole series of other smaller, that is, not fully developed social revolutions in Persia, Sparta, China, which carried within themselves, all the same, in nascent form the same cruel destructive character of the great revolutions.

As for our Time of Troubles, which occurred three hundred years ago, it reminds us of the Russian Revolution only in the common psychology of Russian revolt, but not at all in ideology.

All of its leaders, even those like Bolotnikov, who was the closest to the Bolsheviks in his program, were staunch nationalists, and never dreamed of any kind of "international." Their worldview was easily compatible with contemporary religious and political ideals that, of course, were also quite contrary to the ideology of today's communists, as different as night is from day.

Government appeared on earth only after the fall of the first people. In Eden was not heard the cry of an overseer. Man never forgets that originally he was as free as a king, and that authority over him is a result of sin. If he submits to external authority, understanding that it is instituted by God as a deterrent to the evil diffused throughout the world, he still chews at the reins like a horse or growls at his tamer like a beast, all because of the influence of that same sin.

That which, in cultured nations with their social discipline, is expressed in "legal opposition" to a government, in more primitive cultures—as witnessed by explorers—is expressed in wild orgies during the transfer of power from one group to another. Then, the mass of people goes on a rampage, castigating their former rulers with the most crude accusations and mockery.

We see something similar in the upswing of revolution. It directs its primary attack at those who are in power and does not calm down until it drinks the blood of those who wear the crown, which for the revolutionaries has some kind of sacral meaning. It was not by accident that after the execution of Louis XVI, one woman bathed her breast with his blood, and applied the bloody breast to the mouth of her infant. Others dipped their handkerchiefs and the ends of their spears in the blood of the king-martyr, as Carlyle writes in his *History of the French Revolution*.

Is this not the same thing as the Jews crying, "His blood be on us and on our children?"

Admittedly, the French nation took this blood on itself already after their chosen representatives voted to condemn the king to death. Yes, it is true that this death sentence—so fateful for France first of all—was passed with a majority of only *one* vote. However, nowhere was there an open protest against the execution of Louis XVI, neither before nor after its fulfillment.

Intoxicated, as it were, by this blood, the French Revolution was capable of reducing the entire country to ashes, if only it did not find Napoleon.

What quality drew others to him so irresistibly, not only during his life, but even now, when his name is no more than a historical remembrance? The titanic sweep of his ambitions and his battle with fate, which often tried to hinder them. His stormy life was a single great tragedy, and people are always attracted by the tragic, in which one sees both the weakness and the power of mankind. "I missed my fortune at Jean d'Acre. It was a grain of sand that undid me," he said concerning his disastrous Egyptian campaign. "I would have reached Constantinople, even India … I would have changed the face of the world."

This "grain of sand" in actual fact was the almighty hand of God, whose tool he and his genius were. In some cases, God saved him from danger, especially when he despaired and was close to taking his own life, but at other times, God hindered his success even when it seemed assured.

Born and raised in the fires and storms of revolution, he had a right to say of himself, "I am the Revolution." In him, to the good fortune of France, the unruly spirit of the revolution was incarnate, forcing him to rush from one end of the world to another, forcing him to expend superhuman reserves of energy and nowhere giving him rest. His heart knew neither the warmth of religious faith, nor love, nor joy, nor pity, nor remorse, something easily seen in his dour expression, constantly turned inward. Only the small island of St Helena, constrained by the sea on all sides, could tame his wild nature. Locked there, like a lion in a cage, "tormented by calm," he could consciously survey his unique historical path, and at least partially humble his pride. His stay there was, if not resolution from his tragedy, then at least the pledge of calm in the world, which had been led by him into the state of a storm at sea. Together with him, or, better yet, in his person, the dying force of revolution was imprisoned, in order to expire and fade away with him on the island of St Helena.

There is nothing new under the sun. What we call today's crisis—and what should more properly be called a global catastrophe that could possibly be a harbinger of the end of the world—was equally foreseen by the Slavophiles and their adversaries the extreme Westernizers, even the revolutionaries. These and the others, each from his own point of view, foretold this current twilight of Europe, with its age-old culture. "Repent, repent," called Herzen in a prophetic tone directed at the West, "judgment has come for your world. Europe is sinking like a ship." Tiutchev said something similar, as did Dostoyevsky and Leontiev, foreseeing the fall of contemporary Western culture.

Today, these prophesies have become facts of life.

All who have any kind of subtlety of spiritual hearing can sense the dull underground rumbling that warns of a coming earthquake.

Both Spengler and Rozanov, as well as a host of Russian and European writers, each in his own literary or philosophical language, write "The Apocalypse of our Time."

Rozanov, in his typical way, profoundly and with conviction diagnosed today's spiritual disease: "In European man we see the formation of emptiness in the place of bygone Christianity, and into this emptiness the entire world tumbles." However, the world tries to hold onto the edge of this gaping abyss, revealing, as Spengler has said, a "will to power." An expression of this will is the idea of the superman, prepared, as he claims, by Darwin's theory of natural selection and the philosophy of Schopenhauer. Nietzsche merely gave it its final philosophical formula, while George Bernard Shaw tries to give it a more practical and "contemporary" character. The foolishness into which Shaw involuntarily wanders, and especially the madness of Nietzsche himself, are the natural logical and moral conclusions of any attempts at human self-deification. All such attempts are condemned in all times.

Having "believed themselves out," people have come to total skepticism. "Doubt has torn apart this earth," complains a certain contemporary writer. "We either know too much or too little." The frightening question—"What is truth?"—once again stands before man's consciousness in all its tragic power. Tortured by its searching, mankind once again seeks salvation in a reawakening of religious feeling, which can be suppressed only for a time, but never fully disappears from the heart of man.

However, having toppled their own idols, contemporary society cannot reject them fully. It is not capable of bringing the full sacrifice of self-rejection that true religion requires. Therefore, mankind prefers the true faith's surrogates: the occult, theosophy, and masonic practices. These spread around themselves the twilight of morbid mysticism or religious eclecticism, so typical of every age of decadence, or they are no more than a series of cold philosophical or moral postulates that nourish the mind more than the heart. In such an atmosphere, religion dies in the actual sense of the word "religion," that is, a re-linking between God and man that infuses the whole being of the latter.

Equally unsuccessful was the attempt to create an apotheosis of the human collective, which instead resulted in a profound disruption of the social and governmental order. Desiring to save themselves from impending chaos, today's cultured nations, driven by an instinct of self-preservation, once again seek men of power and throw themselves into their embraces, ready to sacrifice their freedom merely in order to avoid anarchy. I believe that the time is near when people, having lost "the mighty man and the man of war; the judge, the prophet, the diviner, and the elder," will be ready to seize their own brother and say to him, "you have clothing; you be our ruler and let my food be under your roof" (Isaiah 3:2, 6).

The unraveling organism of government searches for a bulwark in the reinvigoration of its ancient pagan absolutism, which suppressed and swallowed up human personality. From the moment that Christ's exalted moral teaching—which raised the significance of each individual person, whose soul is priceless in the eyes of God, and established a harmony between the personal and social principle—began to lose its age-old softening and ennobling influence on the organism of government, only a single, exposed, and cold metal skeleton remains of it, which strives to dominate human thought and to create, in the words of Berdyaev, "a dictatorship of worldview."

In this way, at the same time as religious feeling fades, society lost the vivifying soul that allowed it to keep itself organized.

Estrangement from the uplift of religious ideals, by which true creativity is always nourished, has made even scientific knowledge fruitless, because the foundation of any science, even the most exact, should be religious faith, according to Spengler. This estrangement has devalued and emptied art itself, bringing it down from the stars to the earth.

Today's art has even lost the ideal of true beauty and the source of inspiration and creative energy.

"The new artist," says Spengler, "is an artisan, not an artist."

This breakdown of contemporary art as a result of the weakening of religious inspiration is vividly described by Professor

E.V. Spektorsky in his serious and in many ways instructive paper, titled "Christianity and Culture":

Religion, that song of the cosmos, according to William James, has ceased to be heard in art. And so the greatest period in the history of art has come to a close, an era of the most exalted art that it would not be mockery to call holy.

Today's taste is cultivated in an unfavorable setting that seems to, on principle, reject aesthetics, for industry and trade do not require the aesthetic to survive.

Nowadays, instead of church, architects most often create "works of art" such as hotels, exhibition pavilions, or towers with restaurants and elevators. In times past, the word *fabrika* (factory) used to mean "church." Now the word means nothing but a factory …

This mechanization of dechristianized culture, which Rathenau so extolled, has resulted in a horrifying vulgarization of taste. Art, aesthetics have been almost completely pushed aside by fashion and recreation. Who in our days does not sing the akathist to fashion! Fashion is essentially a rejection of eternity, and even longevity. Fashion is already no longer yesterday, but not yet tomorrow. Fashion is the caprice of some and the slavery of others.

Spengler, as well as Leontiev in his own time, considered such cultural simplification and a "return to nature" nothing more than a screen hiding "a descent from the eagle's perspective to the frog's in important questions about life." Thus, "the old man, day by day, returns to the embrace of nature." Bolshevism, having absorbed all the elements of mankind's spiritual decay, having brought such "simplicity" to its logical conclusion—primitive savagery—is the best example of this decrepitude of modern society. With its typical sincere cynicism, Bolshevism even dares say what others never dared to utter. Is this not why so many people are attracted to it? It is the result of the old psychological law: *similis simili gaudet* (like gives joy to like).

"Wherever the carcass is, there the eagles will be gathered together" (Matthew 24:28).

"Europe, gazing at the Bolsheviks, has become wild again and wants to return to the forest," said Dmitry Merezhkovsky. It doesn't want to think about the truth that Bolshevism is suicide.[92]

Only rarely does one hear sobering voices in Europe; however, popular opinion pays little attention to them.

"What are we doing?" bravely asked a certain famous preacher in London recently. "Having thrown aside all considerations of caution, dignity, and honor, we befriend the enemies of Christ, we walk arm-in-arm with Judas Iscariot, and we affably joke with Pontius Pilate. Why? All because of money, because of thirty pieces of silver."

All of cultural humanity doubtless has some dim perception of the coming disaster, but, as during the time of the Flood, everyone continues to eat, drink, and be merry, oblivious to the danger. The development of technology helps modern man speed up the tempo of his life in order to drown out his inner sorrow, gnawing at his heart. The airplane, from whose height the earth looks like a moving picture, films, in which consist the constant change of momentary impressions, and the daily paper, which is the same film that changes every day before our eyes—these are the three best symbols of modern life. Constant movement is everything. Humanity, tortured by heavy premonition, does not want to stop and reflect on its fate. It rushes to run away from it itself, so to speak, or better yet to escape that abyss of nonexistence that is already attracting it to itself. Having denied Christ, modern culture has condemned itself to destruction.

It has long been noted that nations that forget God become unworthy of living on this earth and, it seems to me, we are once again hearing the voice of Heavenly justice: "See! Your house is left to you desolate ... until you say, Blessed is He who comes in the name of the Lord" (Matthew 23:39).

If the modern world would only wake up, it would realize the necessity of saying, "Lord, to whom shall we go? You have the words of eternal life."

Only Christianity, which saved the world from decay during the decadent period of ancient culture, can once again pour new life into a mankind so spiritually decrepit. Only it has the power to resolve all political and especially social contradictions that ensnare modern society. One cannot create a "mechanism of good," as Professor Kartashev said, something that modern social wisdom vainly seeks. We must remember that history has seen only one perfect social order on earth, and it blossomed on soil made fruitful by the grace of Christ. People lost their passionate attachment to earthly attainments and even lost the distinction between "self" and "other," but only as long as the fire of evangelical love welded them into a single organism with "one heart and one soul," only as long as their entire being rushed upward to the heavenly city.

In this sense, the Church was, and remains to this day, our "socialism," as Dostoyevsky expressed it. Only in the Church can all nations and all of mankind unite in one universal brotherhood, in one body. The Church has a single, life-giving, social principle: the universal social virtue of love. Love is capable of giving more than cold fairness requires; it is capable of giving its own life for others.

In order to create a kingdom of universal harmony on this earth, the Church does not need to descend from its height and to enter the depths of earthly, human interactions. It does not need to divide estates among people, to which it is often called these days. Instead, modern social life, that is, the lifeblood of society, must raise itself above the earth and once again organically enter the religious sphere. Regardless of all global commotions, only one thing remains unmoved—the cornerstone on which Christ the Saviour deigned to establish the entire life of his followers: "But seek first the kingdom of God and His righteousness, and these things shall be added to you" (Matthew 6:33).

His Beatitude Metropolitan Anastasy (Gribanovsky).

APPENDIX

A Life of His Beatitude Metropolitan Anastasy

H is Beatitude Metropolitan Anastasy was the second First Hierarch of the Russian Church Abroad, after His Beatitude Metropolitan Anthony. He was born Alexander Alekseevich Gribanovsky
on August 6, 1873, on the day of the celebration of the Transfiguration of our Lord, in the village of Bratki, Borisoglebsky, Tambov
Oblast. His maternal grandfather (Karamzin) and later his father
were both priests. His father was named Alexei, and his mother was
named Anna.

After finishing the Tambov Theological School, and later the
Seminary, he was sent on a state scholarship to the Moscow Theolog-
ical Academy. At that time, the rector was Archimandrite Anthony
(Khrapovitsky), later Metropolitan of Kiev and Galicia and after his
exile, the Chairman of the Synod of Bishops of the Russian Orthodox
Church Abroad. The Dean of Students of the Academy was at first
Archimandrite Gregory (Borisoglebsky), and later Archimandrite
Sergius (Stragorodsky), who would later become Metropolitan of
Nizhny Novgorod, then Patriarch of Moscow during World War II.

Nearly a year after finishing the Theological Academy, in April
1898, Alexander Alekseevich Gribanovsky was tonsured by Bishop
Alexander of Tambov in the Kazansko-Godoroditsky Monastery of
Tambov with the name Anastasy, in honor of the Venerable Anastasy
of Sinai, whose memory is celebrated by the Holy Church on April 20.
On April 23, he was elevated by the same hierarch to the rank of hier-
odeacon, and soon afterwards to the rank of hieromonk. In August of
that same year, he was invited by the rector of the Moscow Theological

Academy, Archimandrite Arseny (later Metropolitan of Novgorod), to become the assistant Dean of Students at his alma mater, at which post he remained for two years.

In 1900, Hieromonk Anastasy was assigned to be the Dean of Students of the Bethany Theological Seminary, not far from the Trinity St Sergius Lavra, and in July 1901, after the death of Metropolitan Vladimir of Moscow, he was elevated to the rank of archimandrite and became the rector of the Moscow Theological Seminary, after his predecessor Archimandrite Triphon (Prince Turkestanov) was elevated to the episcopate.

After serving for five years in the Moscow Seminary, Archimandrite Anastasy was appointed Bishop of Serpukhov, a vicar of the Moscow Diocese, replacing Bishop Nikon, who was moved to the diocese of Vologda and later became a member of the State Council. The episcopal consecration of Archimandrite Anastasy occurred on the celebration of the Apostles Peter and Paul—June 29, 1906—in the Moscow Dormition Cathedral, and his residence was assigned to be in the Danilov Monastery, where his predecessor also lived.

At his consecration, according to tradition, he prepared a wonderful speech, in which he profoundly demonstrated the "path of true pastorship in Christ" and in a moment of inspired foresight, he predicted the bloody calamities that truly did strike the Russian Church during the years of the Revolution.

The responsibilities of the new Bishop Anastasy, as vicar of the Moscow diocese, included serving in the main Dormition Cathedral, in the Cathedral of Christ the Saviour, and in many other Moscow churches and monasteries. He also visited various parishes in the diocese, as assigned by the Metropolitan, took charge of all the theological schools in the area (both for girls and boys), supervised Law of God classes in the secular schools of the Zamoskvoretsky Region, chaired the Missionary Brotherhood of Metropolitan Peter, oversaw the committees in charge of the ecclesiastical celebrations surrounding the glorification of Patriarch Germogen, the one hundred-year anniversary of the Battle of Borodino, and the three-hundred-year anniversary of the Romanov Dynasty. He also played an active role in various charitable organizations, secular as well as ecclesiastical, and he oversaw the committee for working-class literacy and its publishing house.

Bishop Anastasy served as the vicar bishop of the Moscow diocese for nearly eight years, and together with his years at the academy, he lived in Moscow for nearly twenty years. It is natural to assume that his spiritual outlook was formed under the influence of the many holy places of Moscow and the great hierarch of the Russian Church, Metropolitan Philaret (Drozdov) of Moscow, who was the very image of a true zealot of piety—a genuine ascetic who knew no personal life and who lived only for God and Church, a man of true moral purity, spiritual authority, and indisputable prestige, a brilliant man of action, a giant of oratory and writing, a force of social and moral power. Many of these qualities became typical also in the First Hierarch of our own Russian Church Abroad, Metropolitan Anastasy.

Before the Great War, in May 1914, when the cathedral of Moscow was occupied by Metropolitan Macarius, Bishop Anastasy was assigned to the independent see of Kholm and Liublin, which had become vacant after Archbishop Evlogy became the ruling hierarch of Volhynia. Only a month and a half after his arrival in Kholm, World War I broke out, and this entire area found itself on the front lines. As a result, in addition to his diocesan affairs, Bishop Anastasy spent a significant percentage of his time visiting active troops in the southwestern front, for which reason he was awarded the Order of St Vladimir, second class, and later received an unusual award for a clergyman—the order of the Holy and Right-believing Prince Alexander Nevsky "with swords."

Russian losses in mid-1915 forced Bishop Anastasy to evacuate together with the diocesan administration from Kholm deeper into Russia. Having moved temporarily back to the Chudov Monastery in Moscow, he still often traveled to Petrograd on various business for his scattered flock. He also visited refugees from Kholm in the regions near the Volga River and even beyond the Urals. At the end of 1915, he was assigned to the see of Kishinev, after Archbishop

Platon was named the Exarch of Georgia. In 1916, he was elevated to the rank of archbishop.

Soon after the establishment of a new Romanian front, Archbishop Anastasy found himself once again near the battlegrounds. Again, as before, he often visited the soldiers in the field to give them pastoral guidance and encouragement.

When the fateful year of 1917 began, and nearly all Russian high society, including much clergy, was seized with revolutionary fervor, Archbishop Anastasy immediately recognized the face of the revolution as the face of Antichrist, and firmly stood in defense of the faith and Christ's Church against all attacks, both on the purity of the faith and the centuries-strong canonical order of the Church.

In August 1917, he left Bessarabia to attend the All-Russian Local Council in Moscow. In addition to working together with other bishops in the general business of the Council, he also headed the general services department of the Council and also chaired the committee in charge of organizing the choosing and enthronement of the new patriarch, Tikhon. He described the triumphant rite of enthronement in his article "Choosing and Enthroning His Holiness Patriarch Tikhon, His Personality and Work in the Church." It is not surprising that despite his relative youth—he was only forty-four years old—Archbishop Anastasy found himself among the candidates for the patriarchate, having received seventy-seven votes of the total 309. This clearly demonstrates the respect he commanded. The enthronement of the newly chosen Patriarch Tikhon was brilliantly planned and executed by him, even though by that time the Kremlin was in the hands of the Bolsheviks.

For several months after the enthronement, Archbishop Anastasy remained in Moscow, making himself very useful to the new patriarch in the work of organizing a new ecclesiastical government, in keeping with the decisions of the Council, and in March 1918 he was awarded the right to wear a diamond cross on his *klobuk*. After a reorganization of the structures of ecclesiastical, Archbishop Anastasy became a member of the Most Holy Synod and the Supreme Ecclesiastical Council.

In October 1918, with the blessing of Patriarch Tikhon, he traveled to Odessa with the hopes of reestablishing severed contacts with Bessarabia, which had been seized by Romania. However, he found it impossible to return to Kishinev, because the Romanian government had begun an intense campaign of Romanization and because the secular and ecclesiastical authorities of Romania insisted that he move the entire diocese of Kishinev into the jurisdiction of the Romanian Orthodox Church, which Patriarch Tikhon could not sanction. Archbishop Anastasy himself had no desire to break canonical links with his Mother Church. Rather than living an easy life in a safe place, he chose instead a life of exile amid the waves of revolutionary storm, and eventually far beyond the borders of his fatherland, even so far as America beyond the ocean, together with many thousands of Orthodox Russians, forced to leave their native country.

In connection with the dangerous situation in the south of Russia, Archbishop Anastasy was forced to leave Odessa in 1919 for Constantinople. Having then returned for a brief time to Russia, he visited Novorossisk, Rostov, and Novocherkask, where he came into contact with the Supreme Ecclesiastical Authority, headed by Metropolitan Anthony. In 1920, he once again traveled to Constantinople through Odessa, where he was given the responsibility to oversee the Russian Orthodox parishes in the Constantinopolitan area. The number of these communities had especially grown after the retreat of the armies of General Wrangel and many Russians with him, who did not wish to remain under the yoke of the Soviet government oppressing the country of their birth.

In 1921, sent by the Supreme Ecclesiastical Authority, which had moved from Southern Russia first to Constantinople, then to Yugoslavia, Archbishop Anastasy visited Athos and the Holy Land with the purpose of assessing the situation of Russian monasteries on Athos after the war, and especially the state of the Russian Ecclesiastical Mission in Jerusalem, whose finances completely decimated by the war, which left a heavy mark on the internal life of the Russian women's monasteries in Palestine.

In November 1921, Archbishop Anastasy participated as a representative of the Russian Church in the so-called "Pan-Orthodox Congress" called by Patriarch Meletios (Metaxakis) in Constantinople. This "Congress" raised the questions of the possibility of a new ecclesiastical calendar, second marriages for clergy, married episcopate, shortened services, abolishment of fasting, and simplification of the requirements for priestly garb. Archbishop Anastasy bravely spoke out against all these innovations, all of which were intended to trample on the holy canons—sanctified by centuries of pious tradition in our Holy Church—and, consequently, distorting the very spirit of Holy Orthodoxy. As a result of the subsequent negative change in attitude on the part of the Ecumenical Patriarch to the Russian Church and Patriarch Tikhon in particular—the Patriarch of Constantinople ordered that Patriarch Tikhon be no longer commemorated at liturgy in Russian parishes within Constantinople—and also because he was forbidden to communicate with the Synod of Bishops abroad, Archbishop Anastasy was forced to leave Constantinople after Pascha 1924, and he entered Bulgaria through France, where he took part in the consecration of the Cathedral of St Alexander Nevsky in Sophia, then he moved to Yugoslavia to take part in another Council of Bishops.

The council sent him to Jerusalem to oversee the Russian Ecclesiastical Mission's affairs. Having first visited London to meet with representatives of the English government (who at that time had the mandate over Palestine), he arrived in the Holy Land in December 1924 and remained here for the next ten years, although he traveled once a year to Sremski Karlovci to sessions of the Council of Bishops, and he also visited Patriarch Gregory VII of Antioch in Syria, as well as his successor Patriarch Alexander.

He also traveled to France to meet with Metropolitan Evlogy after the latter left from the jurisdiction of the Synod of Bishops. From Palestine he also made a pilgrimage to Sinai, where Archbishop Porphyrius was then the ruling hierarch.

During the Council of Bishops of 1935, Archbishop Anastasy took part in a special session called by Patriarch Varnava of Serbia for the purpose of establishing canonical communion with the Russian

Church Abroad, which then included Metropolitans Evlogy and Feofil and Bishop Dimitry (Vosnesensky). Metropolitan Anastasy was a representative of the Far East District of the Church Abroad. At this meeting, the so-called Temporary Status regarding the administration of the Russian Church Abroad was formulated.

Archbishop Anastasy was also elevated to the rank of metropolitan by the council and assigned to permanent residence in Sremski Karlovci to be the personal assistant of the already ailing Metropolitan Anthony.

When Metropolitan Anthony died on June 28, 1936, the bishops who assembled to choose his successor could have no doubts about their choice, and Metropolitan Anastasy was unanimously chosen to be the Chairman of the Synod and Council of Bishops of the Russian Orthodox Church Abroad.

The first important work of Metropolitan Anastasy was the reorganization of the Russian Church Abroad, which was divided into four "metropolitan districts"—the Near Eastern, the Far Eastern, the West European, and the North American. During World War II, the Central European Metropolitan District was added to the jurisdiction of the Russian Church Abroad.

In August 1938, Metropolitan Anastasy convoked the Second All-Diaspora Council, consisting of bishops, lesser clergy, and laypeople. The work of the council was then published as a separate book.

Metropolitan Anastasy moved together with the administration of the Synod of Bishops from Sremski Karlovci to Belgrade, since he was also the ruling hierarch of all the Russian parishes in Yugoslavia. He lived on 20 Krunskaia Road, so well known to Russian residents of Belgrade, not far from the Russian Holy Trinity Church, his de facto cathedral, where he spent the first few years of World War II, soon to result in the German occupation of Belgrade and all Yugoslavia.

Every day, Metropolitan Anastasy, a model of strict asceticism, attended the Divine Liturgy at Holy Trinity Church, and the rest of the day, until very late, he was hard at work. Every Sunday and feast day, he served and gave the homily. His sermons were notable for their creative style, their well-formulated arguments, and their multi-faceted subject matter.

Being a devotee of true learning and science—especially theology, of course—Metropolitan Anastasy attracted the best minds, community leaders, and most enlightened clergy of the Church, inviting them periodically to special sessions in his rooms on Krunskaia Road. He established a special Committee of Learning as part of the Council of Bishops, chaired by the former dean of students of the Kiev Theological Academy, Archbishop Tikhon (Lyashcheko), himself a master of theology.

Vladyka Anastasy inspired many with his personal example, and as a result Russian Belgrade led a very intense spiritual life. For example, the "Russian House" held courses in missionary work, intended to combat the rising tide of atheism, religious-nationalist youth groups named in honor of Grand Prince Vladimir, twice-weekly spiritual readings and discussions, and periodic triumphant jubilee feast days. Despite his constant work, Vladyka still found time to take part in all this, attending many meetings, giving direction. In all things, he was the soul of spiritual and philanthropic work.

When World War II began, Metropolitan Anastasy shared its horrors and lengthy deprivations with his flock in Belgrade. The German bombing of Belgrade that began on April 6, which would very quickly seal Yugoslavia's fate, was so unexpected that the capital city found itself completely abandoned by the government as well as many of its residents, who fled in indescribable panic. Amid the general mayhem, only the life of the Russian community in Belgrade continued as it was before the war. The services continued, and priests traveled all over the city, giving communion to the wounded and serving *moliebens* at bomb shelters. During the air raids, Metropolitan Anastasy remained in his place in the altar, while the assigned clergy served *moliebens* before the miracle-working Kursk Root Icon of the Mother of God of the Sign. All this despite the fact that in the immediate vicinity of the church five bombs exploded, the neighboring Serbian church of St Mark was destroyed, and a huge fire raged for two days where a warehouse full of timber exploded. On the second day of this fire, on March 25/April 7, the day of the Annunci-ation, during a particularly violent bombardment, Vladyka stood at a liturgy performed by a priest in the cellar of the Russian House for the many Russians sheltering there. This liturgy, reminiscent of the ancient catacombs, remained etched in the memories of those who communed—all three hundred people, given a special blessing to commune after general confession by the Metropolitan himself—on account of the fatal danger looming over everyone.

In exactly one week, on Lazarus Saturday, the Germans entered the completely destroyed and abandoned city, and the subsequent few years were very difficult for the Russian émigrés in Yugoslavia. Together with his flock, Metropolitan Anastasy braved famine, cold, all manner of constraint and deprivation, various unpleasantness from the occupying Germans, and occasional abuse by Serbians who had succumbed to communist propaganda.

Soon after the occupation of Yugoslavia began, the Gestapo came to do a thorough search of Metropolitan Anastasy's home and appro-priated all the records of the Synod of Bishops. However, they were forced to conclude that Vladyka, as a true Pastor of Christ's Church, remained aloof from all politics, and they left him alone. Somewhat later, they tried to use Vladyka's authority for their own purposes. They offered him to encourage the Russians to collaborate with the Germans in their attack on the Bolsheviks. But despite the fact that in the beginning of the war many Russians trusted the Germans, Vladyka Anastasy refused this offer, because he believed the ultimate motives of German politics to be at best suspicious with regards to Russia.

Metropolitan Anastasy never acted in extreme fashion, but always acted with total dignity, a true High Priest of God. This characteristic was mentioned in London to various ecclesiastical and community organizations by the Serbian Patriarch Gabriel, who underlined that Metropolitan Anastasy acted with great wisdom and tact in the midst of very difficult circumstances, although his residence was searched several times by the suspicious Germans.

In September 1941, Metropolitan Anastasy gave his blessing to the Russian patriots to establish the Russian Corps, hoping that the time had come to free the Russian people from the bloody yoke of Bolshevism. However, the corps was not allowed to participate in the Eastern Front, but was left in Yugoslavia to fight local communist guerillas.

When the Soviet authorities, having found themselves as a result of the war in a critical state, decided to save themselves by appealing to the religious and national emotions of the Russian people, they allowed the remaining episcopate in Russia (eighteen bishops) to have a church council, during which, on September 8, 1943, Metropolitan Sergius (Stragorodsky) was chosen Patriarch of Moscow. Many Russian people were inclined to greet this news with joy. However, an extraordinary session of the Synod of Bishops (eight bishops participated) called by Metropolitan Anastasy in Vienna declared the manner of choosing as completely non-canonical and the consequent impossibility of accepting Metropolitan Sergius as the lawful patriarch.

After Pascha 1944, the English and Americans bombed Belgrade nearly every day, and many people died. Despite the dangers, Metropolitan Anastasy once again did not change his usual manner of living, continuing to serve and preach on all Sundays and feast days, to visit the wounded, to serve funerals for the killed, to comfort the refugees and homeless. He was always very careful to find out if any of his flock had suffered after a raid. The clergy, inspired by their hierarch, visited houses every day with the miracle-working Kursk Root Icon of the Mother of God. Many miraculous occurrences have been written down in connection with these visits.

In September 1944, when the Soviet armies were nearing Belgrade, the majority of Russians fled to Vienna. The Synod of Bishops, its administration, and Metropolitan Anastasy himself also evacuated with the mass of Russian refugees. In Vienna, he did not stop serving in the two Russian churches of the city—the old consular church and a new house church—literally under the bombs of the Allies and in the midst of raging fires. In this city, the miracle-working Icon of the Mother of God also made daily visits to homes and bomb shelters, even visiting some Austrians, who had great respect for this holy object. Again, many miracles occurred as a result of Her visits.

From Vienna, Metropolitan Anastasy moved the Synod first to Carlsbad, then later, already after the end of the war in the summer of 1945, to Munich, which for a time became the largest center of Russian ecclesiastical and social life. In Munich alone (including the surrounding areas), there were about fourteen parishes leading an intense church life, many of them serving liturgies daily. That same summer, Metropolitan Anastasy, together with Metropolitan Seraphim, consecrated Archimandrite Alexander (Lovchy) of Munich as Bishop of Kissingen, vicar bishop of the Diocese of Germany.

Desiring to reestablish communication with the various parts of the Church Abroad severed by war, Metropolitan Anastasy requested and was granted permission to go to Geneva, from where he easily communicated by mail with all the international communities of the Russian Church Abroad, thereby strengthening its fracturing unity.

In Switzerland, Metropolitan Anastasy remained nearly seven months, and during this time he consecrated two bishops together with Bishop Jerome, who arrived from America. Archimandrite Seraphim (Ivanov) was consecrated Bishop of Santiago, and Archimandrite Nathaniel was consecrated Bishop of Brussels and Western Europe.

By Pascha 1946, he returned to Munich, where he soon convoked a council of émigré bishops, which included the bishops of the Autonomous Ukrainian and Belorussian Churches, who were given equal status with the representatives of the Metropolitan Districts. Fifteen bishops were present, while the rest sent letters with their wishes and written opinions regarding the questions to be discussed. This council announced a special jubilee celebration of the fifty-year anniversary of the elevation to the priesthood of Metropolitan Anastasy, as well as the tenth anniversary of his service as First Hierarch of the Church Abroad. The council also bestowed on him the title "His Beatitude," the right to wear two *panagias*, and the right for a cross to be borne before him in ecclesiastical procession (a right reserved for heads of autocephalous churches). But Metropolitan Anastasy categorically refused all these honors, as well as the celebration of his anniversary, saying that it was not the time to celebrate.

And Vladyka remained true to his word: in Munich the anniversary was celebrated, but without the metropolitan, who hid from the honors in his monastery.

After the war, Vladyka's attention was occupied in helping Orthodox Russians evacuate defeated Germany and find new places to live and organize normal parish life. Many new episcopal sees were established in various countries, and many bishops who assembled as a result of the war in Western Germany gradually received new assignments.

In September 1950, Metropolitan Anastasy traveled to the Diocese of Western Europe, where he consecrated Archimandrite Leonty (Bartoshevich) as Bishop of Geneva and blessed a new church in Brussels, built as a monument to the Tsar Martyr and all those killed during the Revolution. Having returned to Germany, he blessed a new Church of the Resurrection in Frankfurt.

Beginning in 1948, many Russians moved to North America, especially the United States, and they began to ask the Metropolitan to relocate the Synod as well. Many Americans also asked the same, especially after the tragic Cleveland Council of 1946, which divided the Russian Church in America, some parishes deciding to submit to the jurisdiction of Patriarch Alexis I of Moscow. At first, Metropolitan Anastasy hesitated, but Munich was becoming gradually more and more empty of Russian Orthodox; many of the DP camps and the parishes associated with them were being closed. Finally, the First Hierarch agreed to the relocation to the United States.

Metropolitan Anastasy moved to America on November 10/23, 1950, by airplane. He was triumphantly met in New York's Cathedral Church of the Ascension.

The next day after his arrival, Metropolitan Anastasy traveled to Holy Trinity Monastery in Jordanville, where he blessed the recently finished stone church in honor of the Holy Trinity, after which he chaired a Council of Bishops, in which eleven émigré bishops participated.

Here, for the first time in the existence of the Russian Church Abroad, Vladyka performed the rite of Consecrating Chrism, which had been previously received from the Patriarch of Serbia.

The residence of Metropolitan Anastasy became the so-called Synodal Dependency, the New Hermitage of the Root in Mahopac, NY, an hour-and-a-half drive from New York City, built on land donated by the well-known Russian philanthropist Prince S.S. Belosselsky-Belozersky.

The arrival of Metropolitan Anastasy into the United States coincided with the schismatic "council" of the American Metropolia, which chose Archbishop Leonty to be the new Metropolitan after the death of Metropolitan Feofil. Our First Hierarch showed tremendous humility in his call to the hierarchs of the Metropolia to unity and peace. However, a meeting between the two sides was fruitless. The hierarchs of the American Metropolia not only did not desire to reestablish the unity of the Russian Orthodox Church Abroad, which they had broken, but they even furthered the division begun by the Cleveland Council by various non-canonical actions, including receiving priests under suspension.

In the meantime, more and more Russians were arriving from Asia to America, and with their arrival more than 100 new parishes were established, all of which wanted to remain within the jurisdiction of the Church Abroad. They were repulsed by the Metropolia's commemoration of a Soviet Patriarch during liturgy, red flags in their churches, the introduction of pews, as well as many more issues that flew completely in the face of true Orthodox piety.

New parishes were built, and Vladyka Anastasy, despite his advanced years, began to travel to serve in various parishes, indefatigably preaching and speaking at various church functions and meetings, impressing everyone with his continued mental acuity and clearness of thinking.

He consecrated several more bishops:

1. Archimandrite Anthony (Sinkevich) to the episcopal see of Los Angeles on August 6/19, 1951
2. Archimandrite Averky (Taushev) to the episcopal see of Syracuse and Holy Trinity on May 12/25, 1953

3. Archpriest Feodor Raevsky, tonsured with the name Savva, to the episcopal see of Melbourne on January 11/24, 1954

4. Archimandrite Anthony (Medvedev) to the episcopal see of Melbourne on November 5/18, 1956

5. Archimandrite Savva (Sarachevich) to the episcopal see of Edmonton

6. Igumen Nektary (Koncevich) to the episcopal see of Seattle on February 26/March 11, 1962.

In February 1952 the metropolitan's residence and the headquarters of the Synod were moved to New York City, where a small building (312 West 77th St) was purchased.

In fall 1953 Metropolitan Anastasy called the second Council of Bishops on American soil, in which sixteen bishops participated. Its triumphant opening occurred in Holy Trinity Monastery, while the sessions were held in the New Hermitage of the Root. Afterwards, bishops' councils were regularly scheduled every three years.

In 1951, Metropolitan Anastasy traveled across the entire North American continent to California, taking with him the beloved icon of the Russian exiles, the Kursk Root Icon of the Mother of God. This first visit to the West was a true triumphal procession. He repeated it every year. The winter Vladyka spent in New York and a good part of the summer in San Francisco. Because of this, a Synodal dependency was established in Burlingame, near San Francisco, and a house church dedicated in honor of All Saints of Russia.

But the greater part of every year Vladyka spent in New York in his residence on 77th Street, where a house church in honor of the Icon of the Mother of God of the Sign was consecrated. He often attended what became traditional and very well-attended church holidays. Among these were:

— Pentecost at Holy Trinity Monastery, its patronal feast
— St Vladimir's day at the so-called St Vladimir's Hill
— Dormition at the convent of New Diveevo, its patronal feast
— St Job of Pochaev (August 28/September 10) at Holy Trinity Monastery

– Commemoration of the Icon of the Mother of God of the Sign, the miracle-working Kursk Root Icon at the New Hermitage of the Root on the Nativity of the Mother of God (September 8/21) as well as the patronal feast of the Synodal Cathedral (November 27/December 10)

For the good of the Church, Metropolitan Anastasy, despite his old age, did not spare himself in the least. And so in 1955, on the day of Dormition, when he was riding to serve in New Diveevo, he was involved in a car accident that only miraculously left him and his fellow travelers alive. But Vladyka did not even allow himself to be driven to the hospital, as was done to his fellow travelers. He insisted on continuing on to New Diveevo and even served a moleben after the liturgy, preceding it as always with a very insightful sermon, in which he used the car accident as a moment of instruction. However, after this accident, Vladyka recuperated for a rather long time before he found himself able to serve liturgy once again.

Having learned of the approaching fifty-year anniversary of his consecration as a bishop, Vladyka's flock decided to establish a special Jubilee Committee to worthily celebrate this notable date. But Vladyka once again refused to bless the work of this committee.

Still, this notable and rare anniversary was celebrated in all the places of Russian exile with triumphant liturgies and celebrations, but without the attendance of the Metropolitan, who refused to participate, as he did in Munich in the previous decade.

To the great sorrow of the First Hierarch, the last years of his life were darkened by events in his beloved California, where the building of a new Cathedral in San Francisco had resulted in a serious scandal. But soon, thanks to the work of Archbishop John (Maximovich), all the difficulties were ameliorated. Vladyka grew more and more ill and weak, he was even taken to a hospital for tests, after which his sickness increased so much that he could hardly walk without help.

Feeling, apparently, that he could no longer physically administrate the Russian Church Abroad, he announced to a council of bishops that he had decided to retire and he offered them to choose his successor.

The Council of Bishops called for this purpose on mid-Pentecost (May 14/27, 1964) chose the Bishop of Brisbane, Philaret (Voznesensky), to be the new First Hierarch, and Metropolitan Anastasy retired, having finally received the unanimous title "His Beatitude" with the aforementioned honors attendant to such a title, which he had so categorically refused only two decades before.

It was a great joy for His Beatitude Vladyka Anastasy to witness the glorification of the Holy Righteous John of Kronstadt, occurring during the same Council. But soon after this, his life began to ebb away, and on May 9/22, 1965, in the evening he reposed in the Lord, surrounded by his admirers in the new headquarters of the Synod at 75 East 93rd St on the corner of Park avenue, donated by the well-known philanthropist S.I. Semenenko, where during the last years of his life the Synodal Cathedral of the Sign was established.

On the day after his death, on Sunday, May 10/23, the diocesan council scheduled for that day was canceled, and everyone hurried to the Synodal Cathedral, where a hierarchical service was solemnized with Metropolitan Philaret officiating. During the entire rest of the day, *pannikhidas* were served for the reposed First Hierarch. Gospel readings, *pannikhidas*, and lines of well-wishers paying their last respects in between regularly scheduled services continued without abating.

On Monday, May 11/24, Metropolitan Philaret served a memorial liturgy together with ten bishops and sixteen priests. After liturgy, the funeral was served, where in addition to the already mentioned eleven bishops, over forty priests served, as well as ten deacons from all over America. Two choirs sang the funeral—the Synodal choir and the choir of the Holy Trinity Monastery with seminarians. The last prayer of absolution was read by Metropolitan's long-time confessor, Archbishop Averky.

After the funeral, the body of the reposed and most of those attending drove to Holy Trinity Monastery, where a place was prepared for the Metropolitan's body under the altar next to the tomb of Archbishop Tikhon of San Francisco and Western America.

In the evening, a hierarchical *pannikhida* was served before his coffin, and on the next day (Tuesday, May 12/25), Metropolitan Philaret served a memorial Divine Liturgy followed by another *pannikhida* with a procession of the body around the Holy Trinity Church three times. Finally, the body of the First Hierarch was laid to rest in the place prepared for him next to Archbishop Tikhon, a hierarch much respected and esteemed by Metropolitan Anastasy.

With the Metropolitan's death, we lost the last representative of the hierarchs of pre-Revolutionary Russia, as well as the last living member of the Most Holy Synod of the Church of Russia, that is, the last bearer of an undisputed and lawful ecclesiastical authority in Russia, chosen on the last freely assembled Local Council of the Russian Orthodox Church in 1917.

—Archbishop Averky

Metropolitan Anastasy pictured with brethren in front of the Monastery of St Job of Pochaev in Ladomirova, Slovakia. The young boy on the far right is the future Metropolitan Laurus (Skurla). The hieromonk sitting to the boy's left is the iconographer and future Archimandrite Cyprian who painted the water-color of birch trees and the oil portrait on the front cover. ca. 1940.

Metropolitan Anastasy pictured at a Synod meeting in New York. The first person visible to the right of the Metropolitan is St John Maximovich. The second person in on the far right is Archbishop Averky (Taushev) the author of the Metropolitan's biography. Photo © 1959 N. Teliatnikow.

NOTES

Part I: Conversations With My Own Heart (Thoughts and Musings)

1. Although not quoted, this phrase is an implicit reference to Pushkin's "The Prophet."
2. (Translation—NK).
3. Thomas Carlyle, *On Heroes, Hero-Worship, and the Heroic in History* (New York: Longmans, Green, and Co., 1906), 20.
4. Cicero. *De Oratore.*
5. This refers to Wisdom of Sirach 39:22 (*For all things were created for their uses*). This translation from the Russian Language Synodal Bible better fits the author's meaning.
6. Johann Wolfgang von Goethe, *Faust: Parts One and Two* (Mineola, NY: Dover Publications, Inc., 2018), 56.
7. Metropolitan Anastasy, having grown up in an economy backed by gold, would have been shocked at the now ubiquitous use of value-less paper instead of hard currency.
8. Ivan Bunin, "At Midnight Hour I'll Stand and Look." (Translation—NK)
9. The title of Alexander Griboyedov's famous play has become an idiomatic expression of its own in Russian.
10. The reference is to a quote by Horace: "Often you must turn your stylus to erase, if you hope to write anything worth a second reading."
11. Wolfgang von Goethe, *Faust*, trans. Bayard Taylor (Cleveland: The World Publishing Company, 1942). Metropolitan Anastasy is mistaken. It is Faust speaking, not Mephistopheles.
12. One of the fables of Ivan Krylov, presumably.
13. "всечеловек"
14. Alexander Pushkin, "Excerpts from Onegin's Travels." (Translation—NK)
15. Gilbert Keith Chesterton, "A Hymn," https://www.chesterton.org/a-hymn-o-god-of-earth-and-altar/, https://www.chesterton.org/a-hymn-o-god-of-earth-and-altar/.
16. Nikolai Berdyaev, "The Philosophy of Inequality." (Translation—NK)

17. Friedrich Schiller, *On Naive and Sentimental Poetry*. (Translation from the Russian—NK)
18. Not that Metropolitan Anastasy needs to be defended, but it should be noted that the year of this book's publication was 1935, when Mussolini's dictatorship brought great relief to war-torn Italy.
19. Arthur Schopenhauer, "Aesthetics of Poetry," in *Select Essays of Arthur Schopenhauer* (Milwaukee: Sentinel Company Printers, 1881), 153.
20. Carlyle, *On Heroes, Hero-Worship, and the Heroic in History*, 81
21. Mikhail Lermontov, "The Angel." (Translation—NK)
22. Blaise Pascal, *Pensées* (New York: E. P. Dutton & Co., Inc., 1958), 58.
23. Pascal, *Pensées*, 62, 51.
24. That is, the "futile glory" (it is the same in the Russian "тщеславие").
25. Pascal, *Pensées*, 46.
26. (Translation—NK).
27. The author cites this quote as coming from the Book of Job. He may be referring to chapter 4; Eliphaz, not understanding why a righteous man suffers, mocks Job.
28. The author gives the citation as 3 Ezra/Esdras 1:21. The Slavonic Bible has a third book of Ezra.
29. Homily 61 on the Gospel of Matthew. (Translation—NK)
30. Mikhail Lermontov, "When, in the Submission of Ignorance ... " (Translation—NK)
31. Mikhail Lermontov, "From Goethe." (Translation—NK)
32. Anton Chekhov, "Gooseberries," in *The House with the Mezzanine and Other Stories*, trans. S.S. Koteliansky and Gilbert Cannan (New York: Charles Scribner's Sons, 1917).
33. (Translation—NK).
34. John Stuart Mill, *Utilitarianism* (London: Longmans, Green, and Co., 1879), 14.
35. Said by Talleyrand of the murder of the Duc d'Enghien by Napoleon. Ebenezer Cobham Brewer, *Dictionary of Phrase and Fable* (Philadelphia: Henry Altemus, 1898).
36. Leo Tolstoy, *The Complete Works of Count Tolstoy, Volume XX*, trans. Leo Wiener (London: J. M. Dent, 1905).
37. In Russian the two words *istina* and *pravda* are more obviously synonymous.
38. Nikolai Gogol, *The Mysterious Portrait*, http://www.gutenberg.org/files/1197/1197-h/1197-h.htm.
39. Alexander Pushkin, "Elegy." (Translation—NK)
40. Alexander Pushkin, *Eugene Oneguine [Onegin] A Romance of Russian Life in Verse*, trans. Lieut.-Col. Henry Spalding (London: Macmillan and Co., 1881) Canto II, strophe XXXI

41. The writer of Ecclesiastes is traditionally identified as Solomon.
42. *Twilight of the Idols.*
43. The author cites 3 Ezra that is apocryphal and appears in Slavonic Bible.
44. Quoted in Charles Platt, *The Psychology of Social Life* (New York: Dodd, Mead, and Co., 1922), 233.
45. The author uses the word *bylina* from Russian epic poetry, usually about the exploits of the *bogatyri*, the "supermen" of Russian folklore.
46. Nikolai Berdyaev, *The Spiritual State of the Contemporary World.* (Translation—NK)
47. St Augustine of Hippo, *Confessions: Book I.* (Translation—NK)
48. (Translation—NK).
49. Ante-Nicene Fathers, Vol III: Tertullian: Part I: Chapter XXXVII.
50. *Timon of Athens.* Act IV, scene 3.
51. The author is paraphrasing a passage from Pushkin's *The Covetous Knight.*
52. World War II began in 1939, four years after the publication of this book in Russian.
53. Friedrich Schelling, *Philosophy of Art*, http://www.finestquotes.com/quote-id-26795.htm.
54. Plutarch [http://quodid.com/quotes/2287/plutarch/painting-is-silent-poetry-and-poetry-is-painting].
55. The author takes this from a collection of quotes about death in Tolstoy's notebooks.
56. (Translation—NK).
57. St Gregory the Theologian, *On Virginity.*
58. Ivan Turgenev, *The Chalice.* (Translation—NK)
59. Gustave Le Bon, *The Psychology of Revolution.*
60. Victor Hugo, *Les Misérables* (London: Hurst and Blackett, Publishers, 1864).
61. Ivan Bunin, *Arseniev's Life.* (Translation—NK)
62. St Ignatius Brianchaninov, *Otechnik* (a collection of sayings from the Holy Fathers). Volume 6 in the complete works of St Ignatius in Russian. (Translation—NK)
63. Alexander Pushkin, *Mozart and Salieri.* (Translation—NK)
64. Piotr Viazemskii, "First Snow." (Translation—NK)
65. Gogol, *The Mysterious Portrait.*
66. Alexander Pushkin, *A Feast During the Plague.* (Translation—NK)
67. Mikhail Lermontov, "The Sail."
68. Carlyle, *On Heroes, Hero-Worship, and the Heroic in History*, 8.
69. Oswald Spengler, *The Decline of the West: Form and Actuality* (New York: Alfred A. Knopf, 1926).
70. Alexander Pushkin, "Hero." (Translation—NK)

71. A Russian word meaning "way of life, culture, manners of a people." Metropolitan Anastasy is here drawing a link between this word and "*byt*'," "to be."
72. Mikhail Lermontov, "Demon."
73. Alexander Pushkin, "To the Poet."
74. Alexander Pushkin, "October 19."
75. Leo Tolstoy, *War and Peace*. (Translation—NK)
76. Alexander Pushkin, "The Rabble." (Translation—NK)
77. This is a paraphrase of lines from Pushkin's "A Poet."
78. Pushkin, "October 19."
79. From "Three Letters to Chaadaev." (Translation—NK)
80. Alexander Pushkin, "The Village." (Translation—NK)
81. The author most likely means Roger Bacon OFM. (Translation—NK)
82. St John Climacus, *The Ladder*. Step 26. (Translation—NK)
83. Nikolai Gumilev, "Fra Beato Angelico." (Translation—NK)
84. Taken from the summary of the Fourth Conference of Russian Academicians Abroad. Part 1, pages 241, 248, 249.
85. Carlyle, *On Heroes, Hero-Worship, and the Heroic in History*, 152–153.
86. The Russian word is "zhrets," a priest of pagan rites, not "sviashchennik," or "priest" in the traditional sense.

Part II: Essays on Revolution

87. John Milton, *Paradise Lost*. Books I, II.
88. Питирим Сорокин, *Современное состояние России*. Стр. 105. (Translation—NK)
89. (Translation—NK).
90. A compilation of quotes from the fathers as well as passages from their lives. Volume VI in the collected works in Russian.
91. (Translation—NK).
92. *Царство Антихриста*. 195.

SUBJECT INDEX

SCRIPTURE INDEX

The Old Testament